THE
ENCYCLOPEDIA
— OF —
awesome
MACHINES

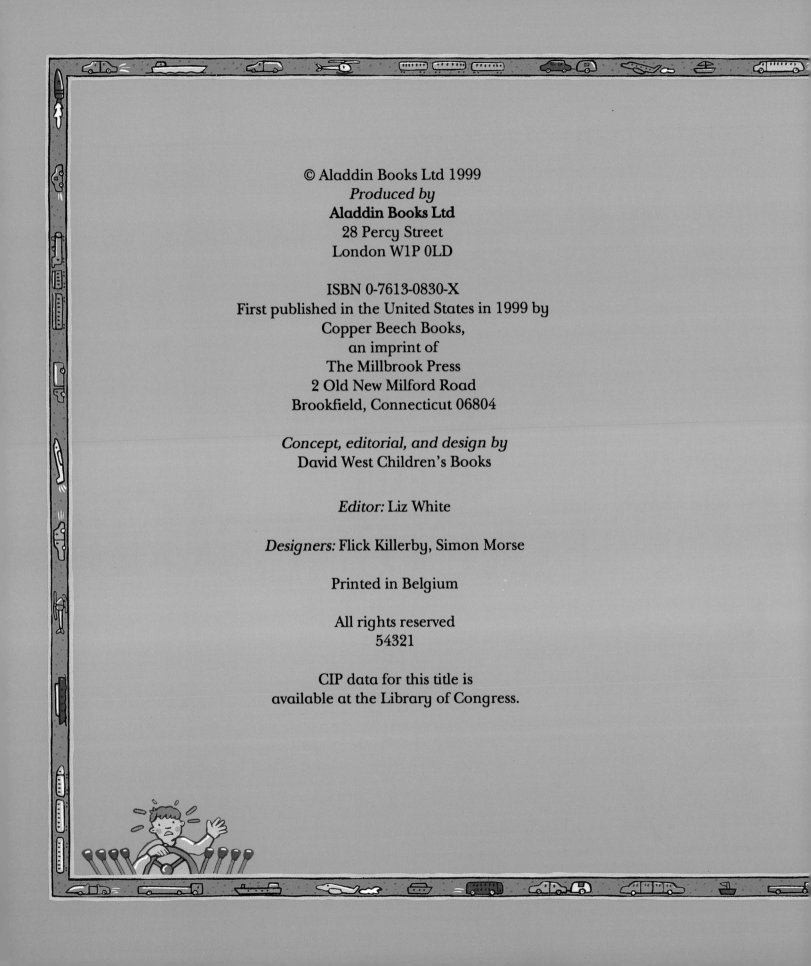

© Aladdin Books Ltd 1999
Produced by
Aladdin Books Ltd
28 Percy Street
London W1P 0LD

ISBN 0-7613-0830-X
First published in the United States in 1999 by
Copper Beech Books,
an imprint of
The Millbrook Press
2 Old New Milford Road
Brookfield, Connecticut 06804

Concept, editorial, and design by
David West Children's Books

Editor: Liz White

Designers: Flick Killerby, Simon Morse

Printed in Belgium

CIP data for this title is
available at the Library of Congress.

THE
ENCYCLOPEDIA
OF
awesome
MACHINES

COPPER BEECH BOOKS
BROOKFIELD, CONNECTICUT

Contents

Introduction

Discover for yourself the most amazing facts about awesome machines from trucks that can swim to boats that can fly and trains that run on one rail.

Chapter by chapter this book will keep you informed about all types of awesome machines. Learn how planes can change shape and how steam trains run on water. Discover all about boats that sink on purpose and cars that have wings. Find out about airships, helicopters, speeding trains, streetcars, warships, cruise liners, tankers, fire trucks, and fast cars. With all these topics to read about, the *Encyclopedia of Awesome Machines* introduces you to some really awesome machines.

Watch for this symbol that means there is a fun project for you to try.

Is it true or is it false? Watch for this symbol and try to answer the question before reading on for the answer.

Don't forget to check the borders for extra amazing facts.

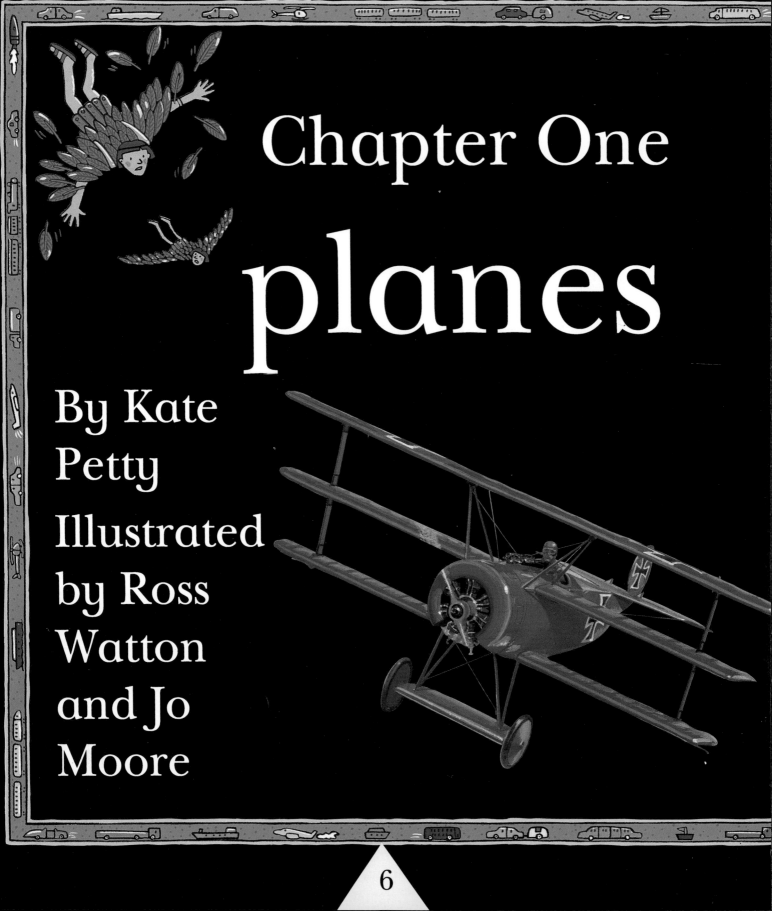

Chapter One

planes

By Kate
Petty

Illustrated
by Ross
Watton
and Jo
Moore

Introduction

Discover for yourself the most amazing facts about flying machines, from the earliest planes to the latest computer-controlled machines that can change shape as they fly.

Did you know that airships contain no air? ... that some planes fly without engines? ... that some planes had three wings? ... that planes can land on water?

... that a *Comet* was the first jet airliner? ... that some planes are rocket-powered? ... that planes can change shape? ... that some planes hover?

I didn't know that

airships contain no air – well, not air as we know it. Some gases are lighter than air even without being heated. The first airships were filled with hydrogen gas. They were powered by engines and could be steered.

The *Hindenburg* burst into flames in 1937. During World War II, hydrogen-filled barrage balloons were tethered over London. Enemy planes caught fire when they flew into them or into the cables that tethered them.

The first airship, flown by Henri Giffard in 1852, was steam-powered.

Modern airships are filled with helium gas. Helium gas is lighter than air but it won't catch fire. This airship (right) can carry 20 passengers. It uses swiveling *propellers* to help it steer, take off, and land.

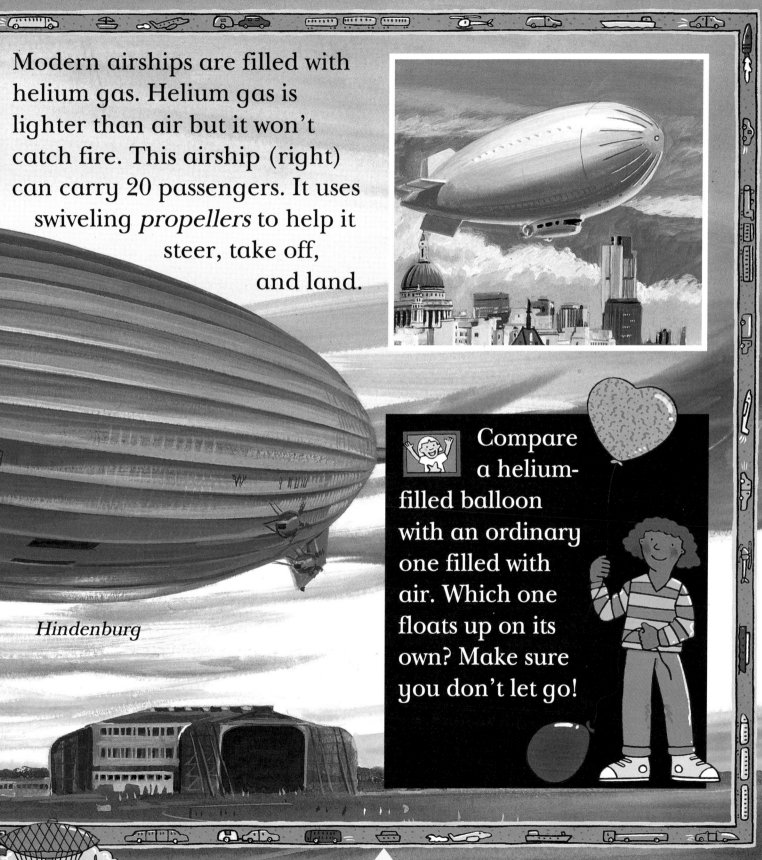

Hindenburg

Compare a helium-filled balloon with an ordinary one filled with air. Which one floats up on its own? Make sure you don't let go!

 True or false?

The Space Shuttle is a glider.

Answer: **True**

When the Space Shuttle reenters the earth's atmosphere on its way home, it glides halfway around the world before it comes in to land.

Glider

Many of the first "heavier-than-air" flying machines that were tested in the early 1900s were gliders. The Wright brothers experimented with gliders for four years before their first powered flight in 1903.

In 1849, a triplane glider lifted a ten-year-old boy into the air.

I didn't know that

some planes fly without engines. Once a glider has been towed into the air it uses rising currents of hot air (thermals) to gain height. The curved shape of the wings keeps the glider airborne as it moves forward.

SEARCH & FIND & FIND & SEARCH &

Can you find the gliding seagull?

The German aviator Otto Lilienthal (right) made well over 2,000 glides before crashing to his death in 1896. His gliders were very similar to modern hang gliders.

Hang glider

I didn't know that

some planes had three wings. *Biplanes* and triplanes get strength and *lift* from their wings. This can make them more tough and maneuverable than monoplanes.

The *Phillips Multiplane* of 1907 had 200 narrow, slatlike wings. Its designer, Horatio Phillips, gave it up after a few disappointing tests.

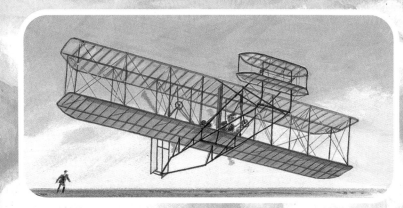

The Wright brothers' first powered flight in 1903 was in a biplane. They had spent many months making an engine that would be light enough.

Can you find the *Bleriot* monoplane?

SEARCH & FIND SEARCH & FIND

Fokker DRI

Vickers-Vimy Biplane

True or false?

A biplane was the first plane to cross the Atlantic Ocean.

Answer: **True**

It was a *Vickers -Vimy Biplane* flown by British pilots Alcock and Brown in 1919.

Lindbergh crossed the Atlantic solo from New York to Paris in 1927.

I didn't know that

planes can land on water.

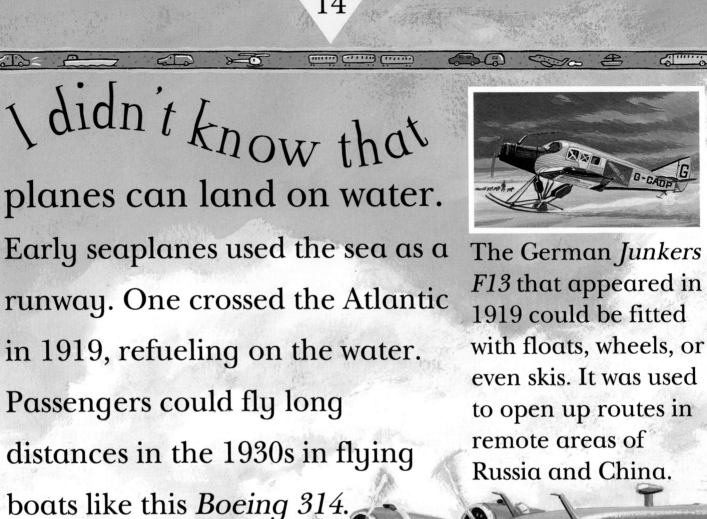

Early seaplanes used the sea as a runway. One crossed the Atlantic in 1919, refueling on the water. Passengers could fly long distances in the 1930s in flying boats like this *Boeing 314*.

The German *Junkers F13* that appeared in 1919 could be fitted with floats, wheels, or even skis. It was used to open up routes in remote areas of Russia and China.

The first airmail services started in Australia in 1914 and in the U.S. in 1918. Flying boats were later used to increase the overseas service.

Boeing 314

The wooden *Spruce Goose* was the largest seaplane ever. It only flew once.

The latest flying boat is the *Sea Wing* (right), made in Tasmania. It is actually a boat, but it takes off from the water and flies above the water at a speed of 160 knots. It is especially good at flying in rough, stormy weather.

AMERICAN AIRWAYS SYSTEM

True or false?
The first seaplane flew in 1910.

Answer: **True**
Henri Fabre took off from a lake in the seaplane *Canard*. He flew for one mile, just 13 feet above the water.

I didn't know that

a *Comet* was the first *jet* airliner. In 1952, passengers were thrilled by their fast, comfortable flight from England to South Africa in the new British-designed jet. Later, the *Boeing 707* became more popular as a commercial airliner.

SEARCH & FIND

Can you find the pilot?

FIND & SEARCH

The first encounter between high-speed, jet-powered craft took place in 1944 when a British *Gloster Meteor* intercepted a pilotless *Doodlebug* (German V1 flying bomb) over London.

Comet

The smallest jet plane, the *Silver Bullet*, weighs about as much as three people.

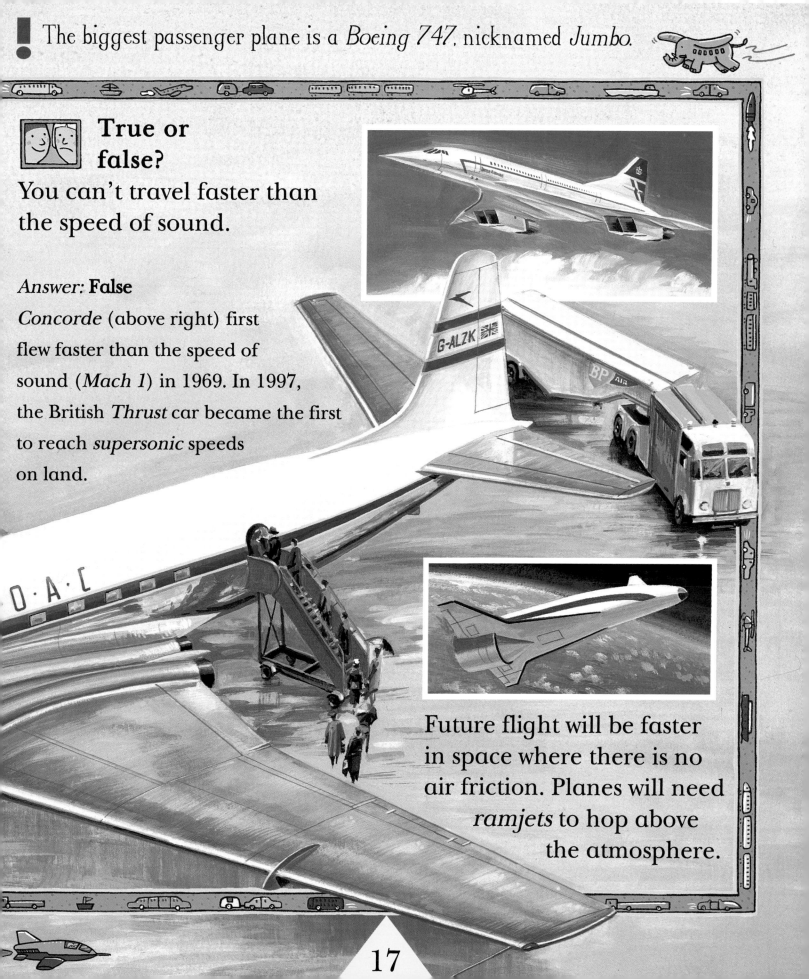

True or false?

You can't travel faster than the speed of sound.

Answer: **False**

Concorde (above right) first flew faster than the speed of sound (*Mach 1*) in 1969. In 1997, the British *Thrust* car became the first to reach *supersonic* speeds on land.

Future flight will be faster in space where there is no air friction. Planes will need *ramjets* to hop above the atmosphere.

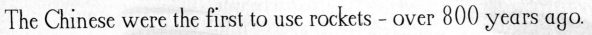 
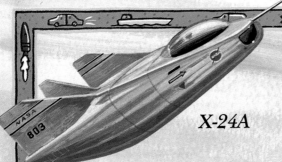

X-24A

 True or false?

Planes have to have wings to fly.

Answer: **False**
This *X-24A* was used for NASA research into a plane that got its lift from the shape of the whole body and not just the wing. In 1970, it flew at 781 mph (Mach 1.19).

I didn't know that

some planes are rocket-powered. Liquid-fueled rocket engines power the fastest planes. The *X-15*s were experimental aircraft. In 1967, the *X-15 A-2* reached 4,507 mph (Mach 6.86).

Chuck Yeager was the first pilot ever to go supersonic. In 1947, he flew in a *Bell X-1* at 670 mph (Mach 1.015).

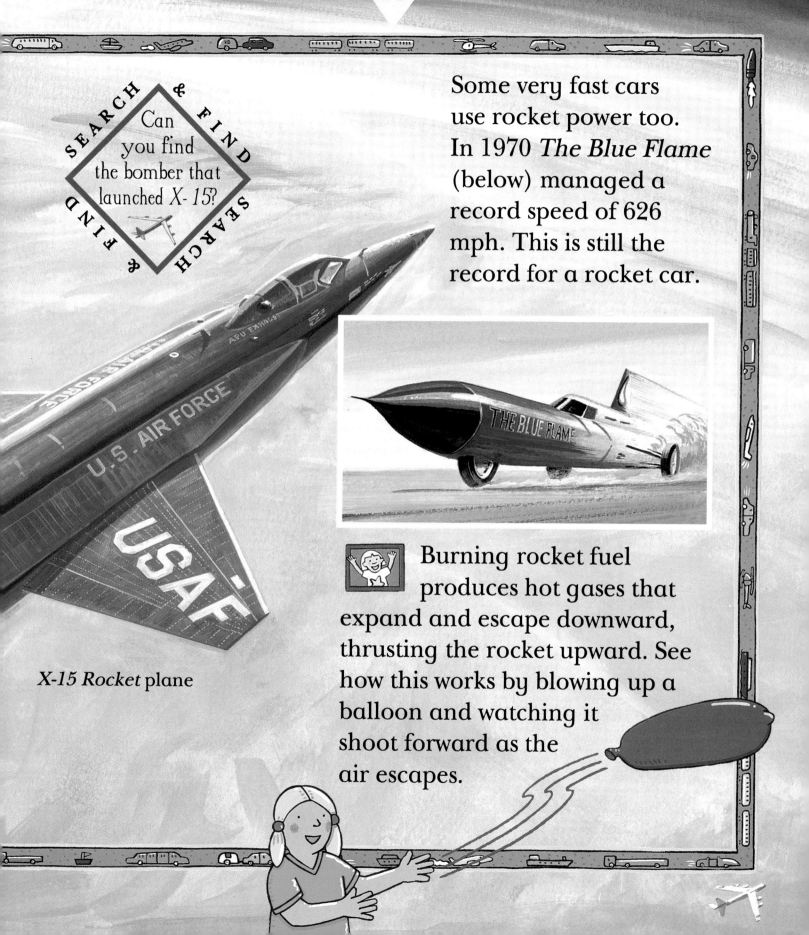

SEARCH & FIND & SEARCH & FIND Can you find the bomber that launched X-15?

Some very fast cars use rocket power too. In 1970 *The Blue Flame* (below) managed a record speed of 626 mph. This is still the record for a rocket car.

THE BLUE FLAME

Burning rocket fuel produces hot gases that expand and escape downward, thrusting the rocket upward. See how this works by blowing up a balloon and watching it shoot forward as the air escapes.

X-15 Rocket plane

I didn't know that

planes can change shape.

Some modern planes, like the *Panavia Tornado*, can change shape in midair. Others have a variety of wing designs, with wings fixed in different shapes and positions.

Lockheed F-117 Stealth fighter

 True or false?
Planes can be invisible.

Answer: **True**
The unusual-looking *Lockheed F-117 Stealth* fighters are designed to absorb or deflect *radar* signals, which means that they don't show up on radar screens.

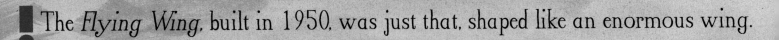
The *Flying Wing*, built in 1950, was just that, shaped like an enormous wing.

Panavia Tornado with wings swept back.

Some new aircraft look back-to-front! The wings on this NASA *X-29* (above) face forward to help the plane turn tight corners at high speed.

Panavia Tornado with wings extended outward.

The fastest jet-powered aircraft was the *Lockheed SR-71* (right), a spy plane called *Blackbird*. It flies at high speeds and altitudes to avoid detection.

The autogiro can't hover. Its main *rotor* has no engine to power it. The engine only powers the propeller which drives the autogiro forward. The rotor then rotates in the wind and produces lift.

Apache AH-64

Look for natural helicopters! Some tree seeds are dispersed with "rotors." Watch sycamore or ash seeds as they spin away from the tree on the wind.

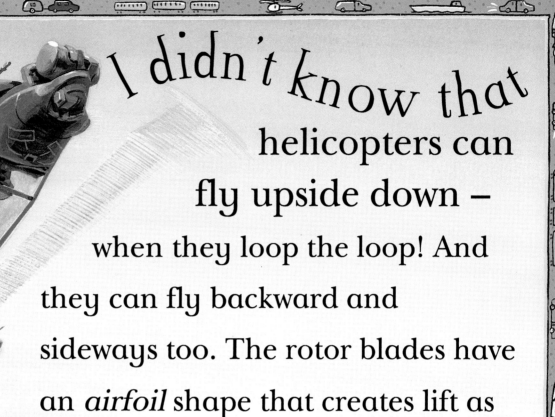

I didn't know that helicopters can fly upside down – when they loop the loop! And they can fly backward and sideways too. The rotor blades have an *airfoil* shape that creates lift as they rotate.

Helicopters can move vertically and hover, so they're very useful for rescuing people from a tight spot – such as a busy town, a mountain peak, or a stormy sea.

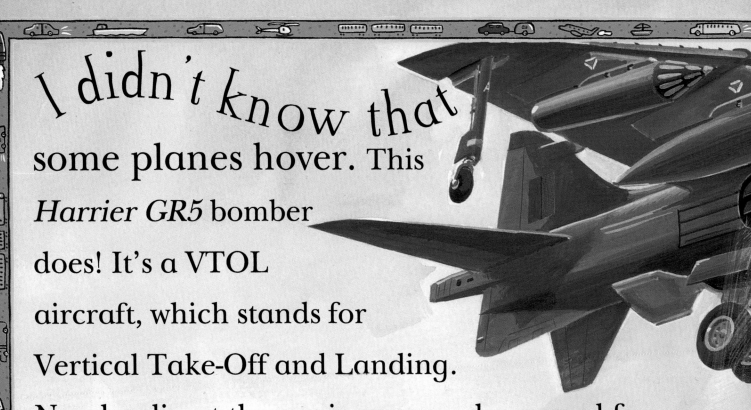

I didn't know that

some planes hover. This *Harrier GR5* bomber does! It's a VTOL aircraft, which stands for Vertical Take-Off and Landing. Nozzles direct the engine power downward for taking off and hovering, or backward for flying forward.

This *Osprey* is a strange bird – a cross between a plane and a helicopter! The rotors are upright for vertical takeoff and then tilt forward for normal flight.

Planes that can take off and land at a steep angle are useful in built-up city areas. This little *DASH-7* is landing at a busy city airport. It is a STOL plane – Short Take-Off and Landing.

Harrier jump-jet

Now humans can hover with a flying belt! A jet of superheated air rushes downward from a jet-pack, thrusting the person off the ground – but only for 28 seconds!

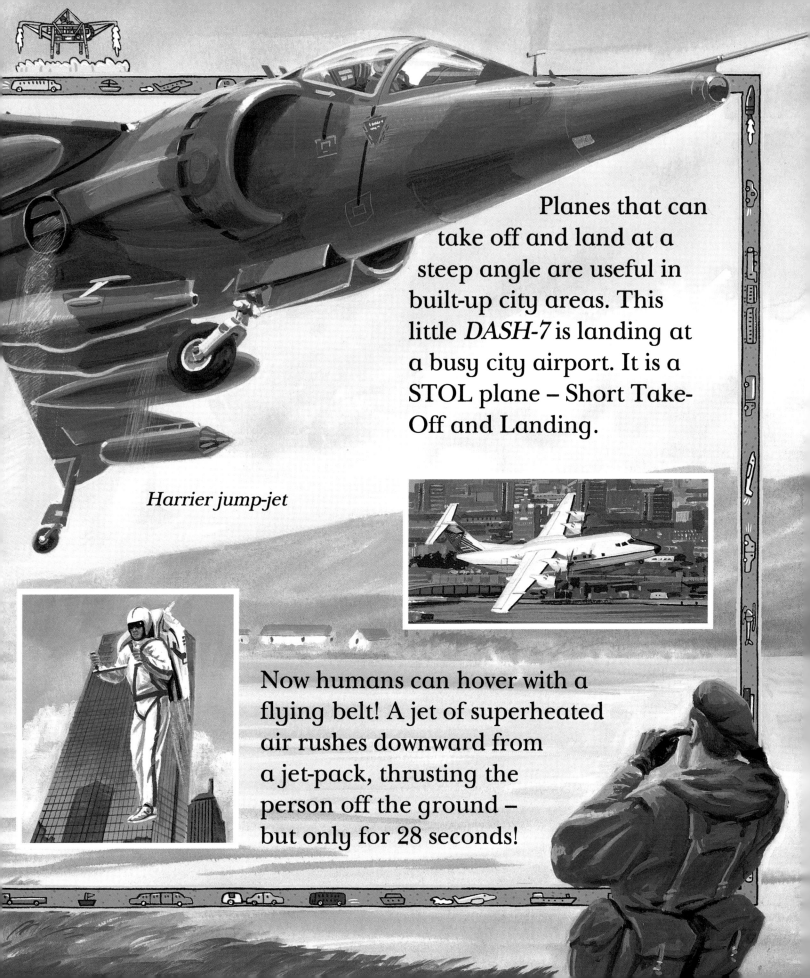

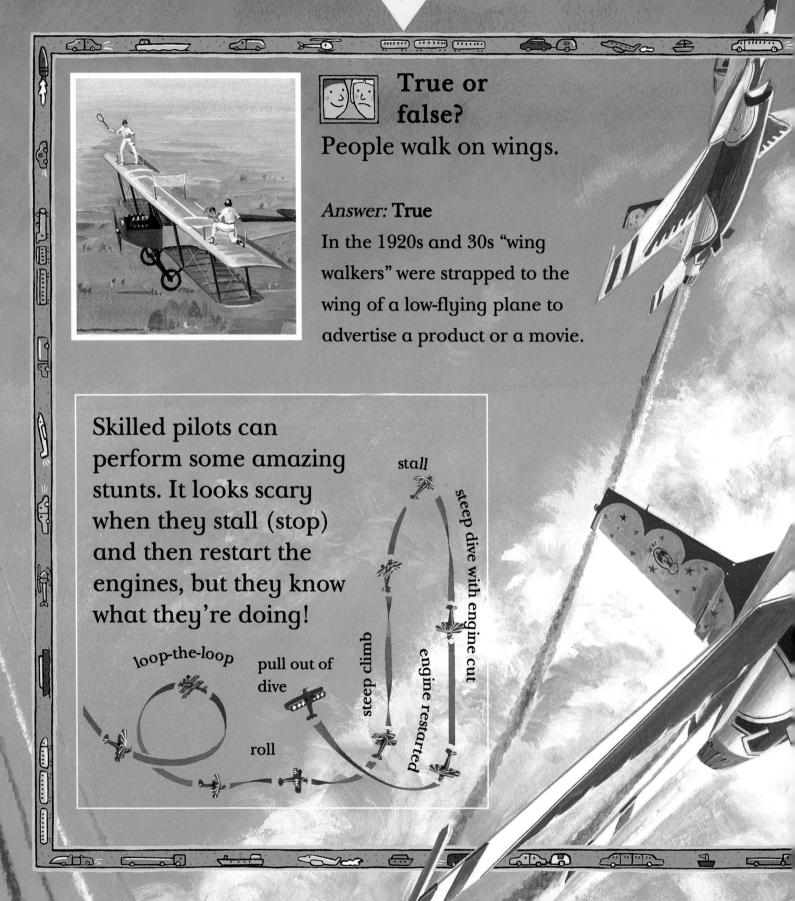

True or false?
People walk on wings.

Answer: **True**
In the 1920s and 30s "wing walkers" were strapped to the wing of a low-flying plane to advertise a product or a movie.

Skilled pilots can perform some amazing stunts. It looks scary when they stall (stop) and then restart the engines, but they know what they're doing!

stall

steep dive with engine cut

engine restarted

steep climb

loop-the-loop

pull out of dive

roll

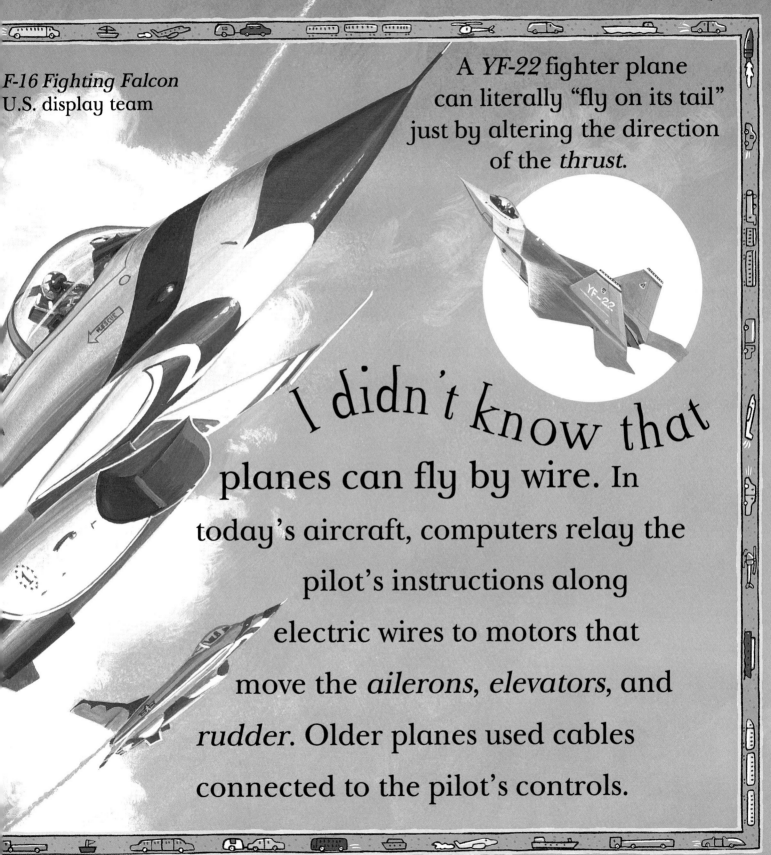

F-16 Fighting Falcon
U.S. display team

A *YF-22* fighter plane can literally "fly on its tail" just by altering the direction of the *thrust*.

I didn't know that

planes can fly by wire. In today's aircraft, computers relay the pilot's instructions along electric wires to motors that move the *ailerons*, *elevators*, and *rudder*. Older planes used cables connected to the pilot's controls.

27

Chapter Two
trains

By Kate Petty

Illustrated by Ross Watton and Jo Moore

Introduction

Discover for yourself amazing facts about rail transport, from the earliest steam trains to the latest high-speed supertrains.

Did you know that steam trains run on water? ... that the biggest steam locomotive had 24 wheels? ... that the *Flying Hamburger* was a train? ... that some trains have several locomotives? ... that some trains don't make their own power? ... that high-speed trains cruise at 185 mph? ... that some trains run on only one rail? ... that streetcars run on the road?

I didn't know that

steam trains run on water.

A steam engine uses water to get its power. A coal fire heats the water. The boiling water turns to steam. The steam is forced into the *cylinders* where *pistons* are pushed that turn the wheels.

SEARCH & FIND
Follow the blue arrows to find where the water goes.

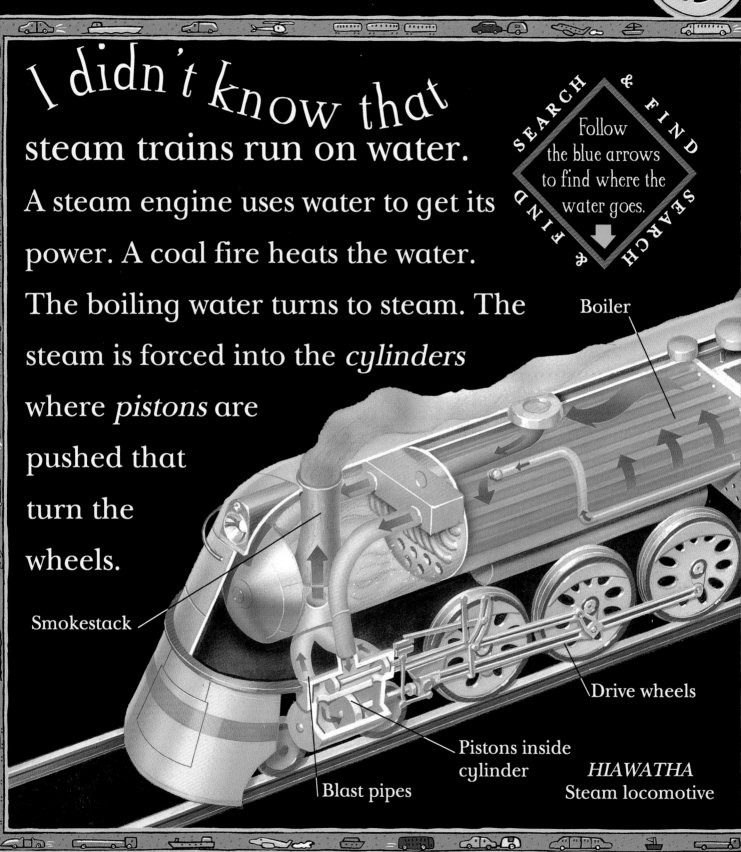

Boiler

Smokestack

Drive wheels

Pistons inside cylinder

Blast pipes

HIAWATHA
Steam locomotive

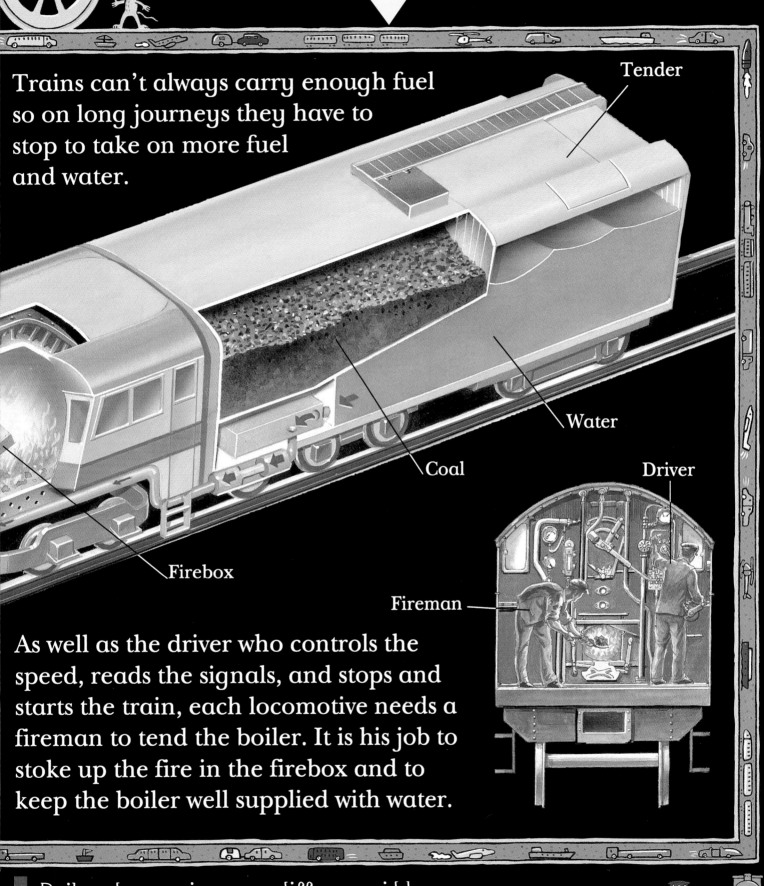

Trains can't always carry enough fuel so on long journeys they have to stop to take on more fuel and water.

Tender

Water

Coal

Driver

Firebox

Fireman

As well as the driver who controls the speed, reads the signals, and stops and starts the train, each locomotive needs a fireman to tend the boiler. It is his job to stoke up the fire in the firebox and to keep the boiler well supplied with water.

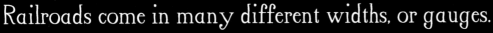

Railroads come in many different widths, or gauges.

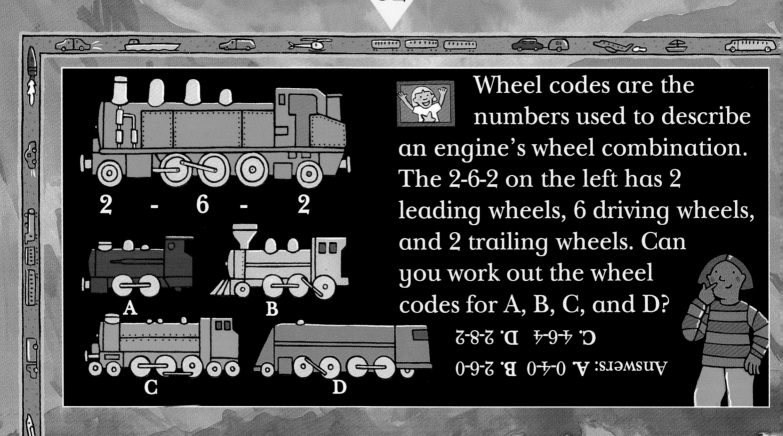

Wheel codes are the numbers used to describe an engine's wheel combination. The 2-6-2 on the left has 2 leading wheels, 6 driving wheels, and 2 trailing wheels. Can you work out the wheel codes for A, B, C, and D?

2 - 6 - 2

A

B

C

D

Answers: A. 0-4-0 B. 2-6-0 C. 4-6-4 D. 2-8-2

UNION PACIFIC

4019

MALLARD

Nº 4468

Mallard was a famous streamlined British steam engine. It set the steam speed record of 125 mph in 1938. This record has never been broken since!

One of the longest trains ever pulled 500 cars of coal.

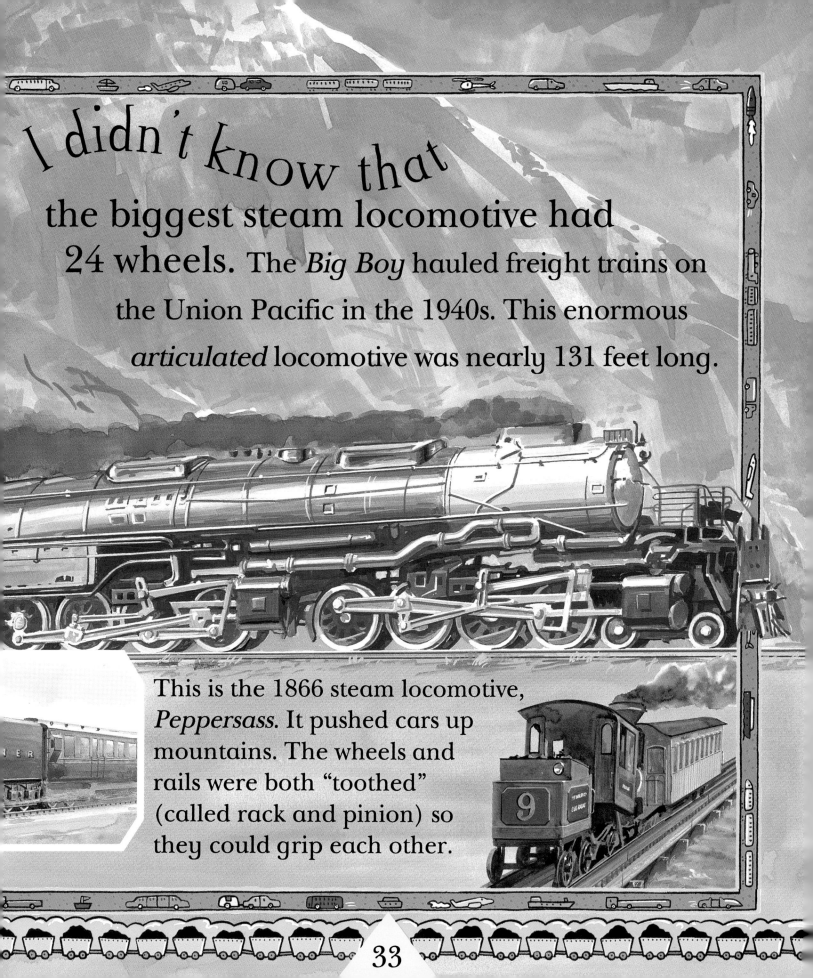

I didn't know that

the biggest steam locomotive had 24 wheels. The *Big Boy* hauled freight trains on the Union Pacific in the 1940s. This enormous *articulated* locomotive was nearly 131 feet long.

This is the 1866 steam locomotive, *Peppersass*. It pushed cars up mountains. The wheels and rails were both "toothed" (called rack and pinion) so they could grip each other.

I didn't know that

the *Flying Hamburger* was a train. In 1933 this German *diesel-electric* two-unit railcar ran at an average speed of 77 mph – proving just how efficient this type of engine could be.

SEARCH & FIND Can you find the hamburger?

FLYING HAMBURGER
Two-unit railcar

Most diesel locomotives are in fact diesel-electric, in which the diesel engine makes the electric power to drive the wheels.

True or false?
Some trains had propellers.

Answer: **True**
A diesel engine powered the propeller at the back of the German *Kruckenburg*. It broke the world record in 1931 with an average speed of 143 mph over 6 miles.

The *Kitson-Still* of 1924 (right) was diesel driven, but the heat from the diesel engine also heated water to produce steam – for that extra push!

! Diesel trains began to be used in the U.S. in 1934.

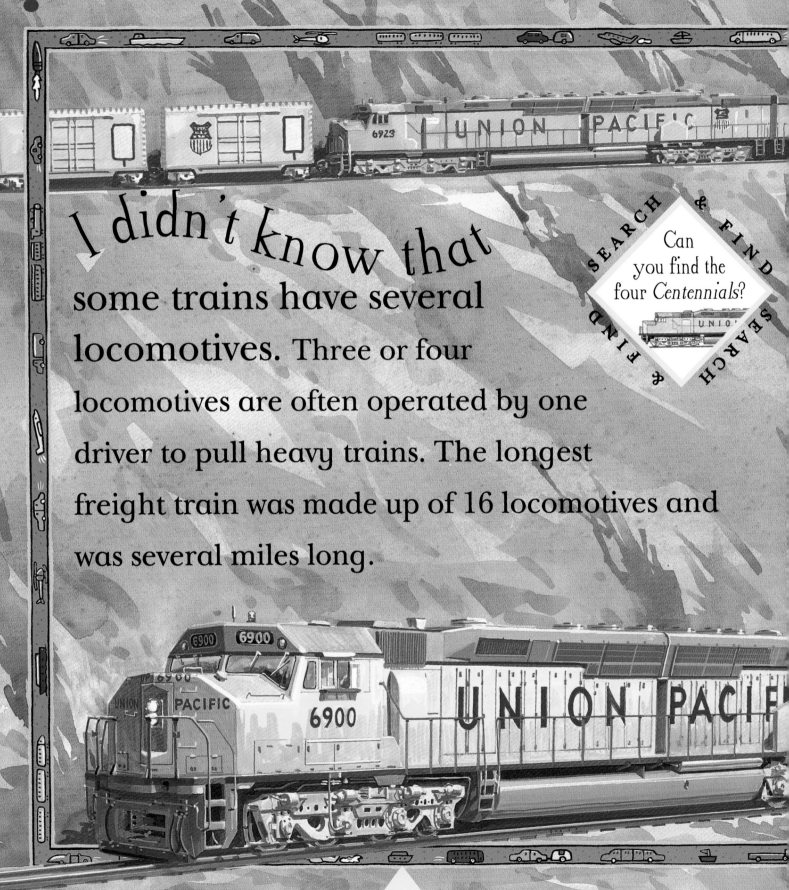

I didn't know that

some trains have several locomotives. Three or four locomotives are often operated by one driver to pull heavy trains. The longest freight train was made up of 16 locomotives and was several miles long.

SEARCH & FIND

Can you find the four *Centennials*?

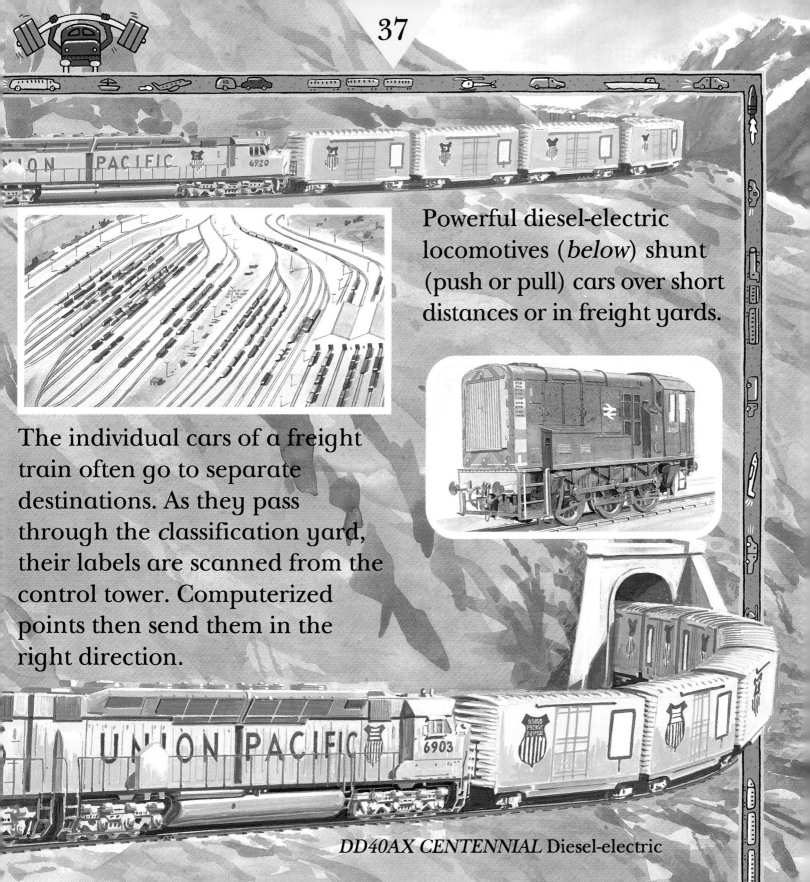

Powerful diesel-electric locomotives (*below*) shunt (push or pull) cars over short distances or in freight yards.

The individual cars of a freight train often go to separate destinations. As they pass through the *classification yard*, their labels are scanned from the control tower. Computerized points then send them in the right direction.

DD40AX CENTENNIAL Diesel-electric

Union Pacific celebrated their 100 years with their new *Centennial* 100

I didn't know that

some trains don't make their own power. Some electric trains get their power from overhead wires via a metal *pantograph* on the roof, others from a *conductor rail* on the ground.

SEARCH & FIND
Can you find the steam engine?
FIND & SEARCH

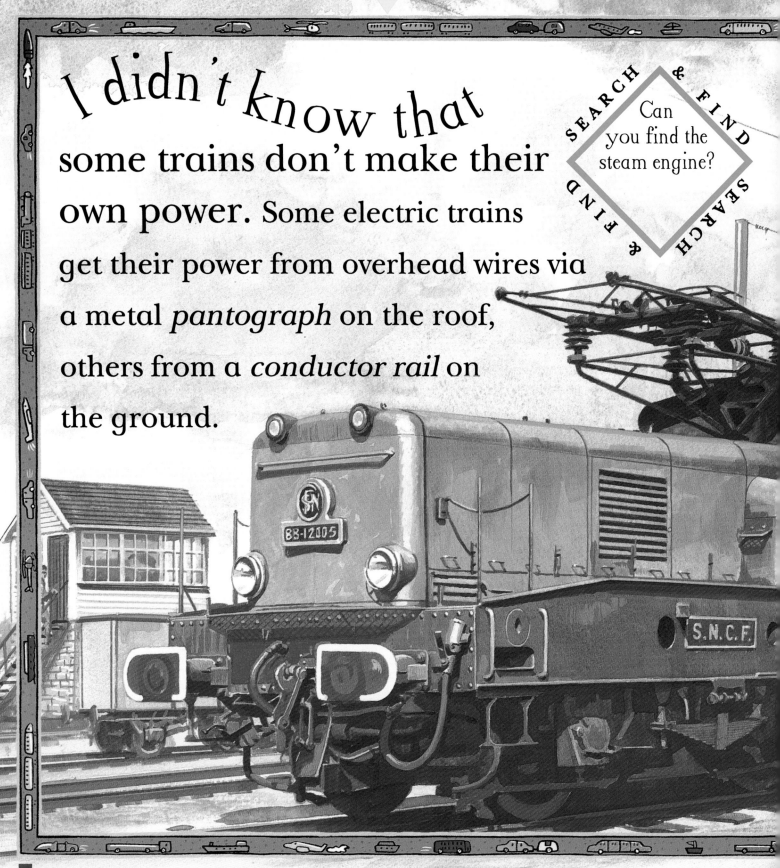

In 1883, Britain's first electric railroad ran along the seafront in Brighton, England.

The *Regio Runners* in Holland (right) are double-decker inter-city trains, powered from overhead electric wires.

French *CLASS 12000* Electric locomotive

True or false?

There were electric trains more than one hundred years ago.

Answer: **True**

Werner von Siemens (*below*) gave a demonstration of his electric locomotive in Berlin in 1879.

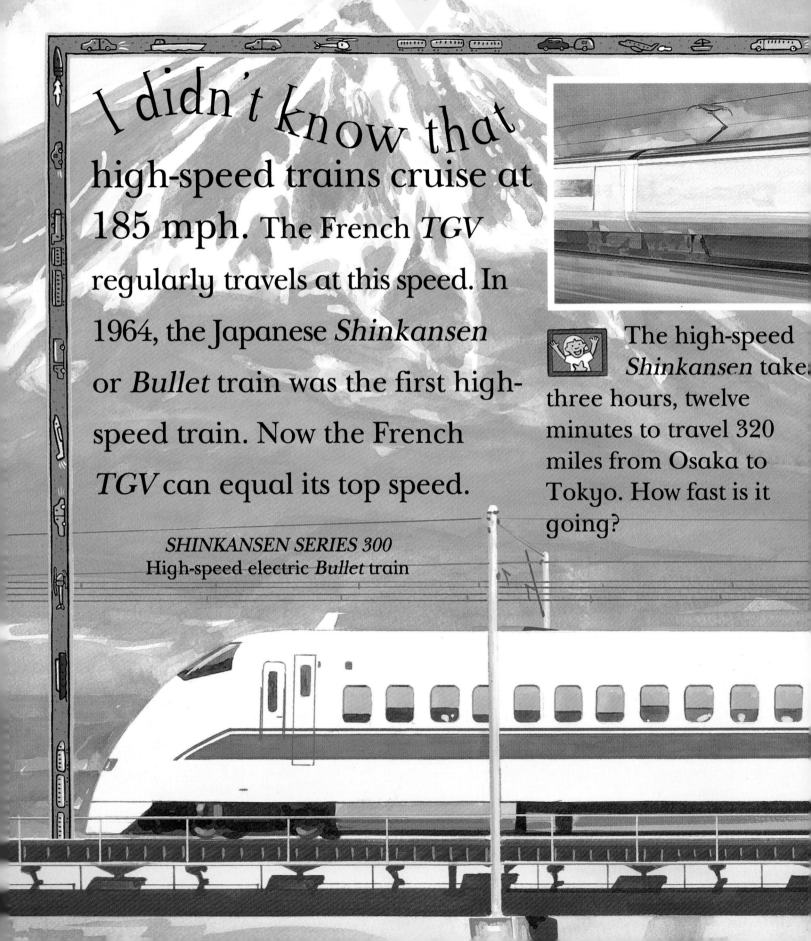

I didn't know that

high-speed trains cruise at 185 mph. The French *TGV* regularly travels at this speed. In 1964, the Japanese *Shinkansen* or *Bullet* train was the first high-speed train. Now the French *TGV* can equal its top speed.

SHINKANSEN SERIES 300
High-speed electric *Bullet* train

The high-speed *Shinkansen* takes three hours, twelve minutes to travel 320 miles from Osaka to Tokyo. How fast is it going?

Eurostar speeds from London to Paris in three hours. It goes under the English Channel from Folkestone to Calais in only 19 minutes. It is a British design based on the *TGV*.

 True or false?

Some high-speed trains lean over when they go around corners.

Answer: **True**

Trains that lean into curves like a cyclist on a bicycle can go faster around bends. Computers on the Italian *ETR* and the Swedish *X2000* (below) tell the train how far to lean as it goes around the bends.

I didn't know that

some trains run on only one rail. A monorail train rides either above or below a single rail. Two vertical wheels guide it along the track and horizontal wheels grip the sides. Sydney's monorail is built on stilts.

The Ballybunion Line in Ireland was a monorail system from 1888-1924. Invented by a Frenchman, Charles Lartigue, the double engine rode on an A-shaped line.

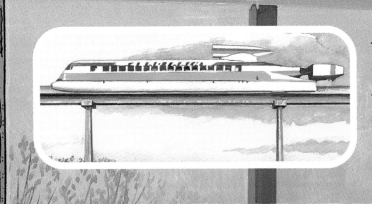

A train with no wheels! *TACV* stands for "tracked air cushion vehicle" – a hovercraft on rails. This experimental Aérotrain is powered by a jet plane's engine.

The power of electromagnets can lift a train above the tracks so that it runs without friction, like this *Maglev* train. If you experiment with two ordinary magnets you will discover just how strong their pulls (attraction) and pushes (repulsion) can be.

A *MAGLEV* in Birmingham, England

Sydney, Australia's *AEG von Roll* monorail

I didn't know that

streetcars run on rails in the road. They travel with overhead wires for power. They are popular because they produce less pollution than buses or cars.

Sheffield's Supertram system, England.

44

Not all trains look like trains. This railcar, built in 1932 for the County Donegal Joint Railways in Ireland, looks much more like a bus!

 True or false?

The cars on a cable railroad have electric engines.

Answer: **False**

The famous cable cars in San Francisco are pulled along by a moving loop of steel cable. The cable runs along a slot in between the rails and the cars clamp onto it.

A diesel railcar in County Donegal, Ireland clocked up nearly one million miles.

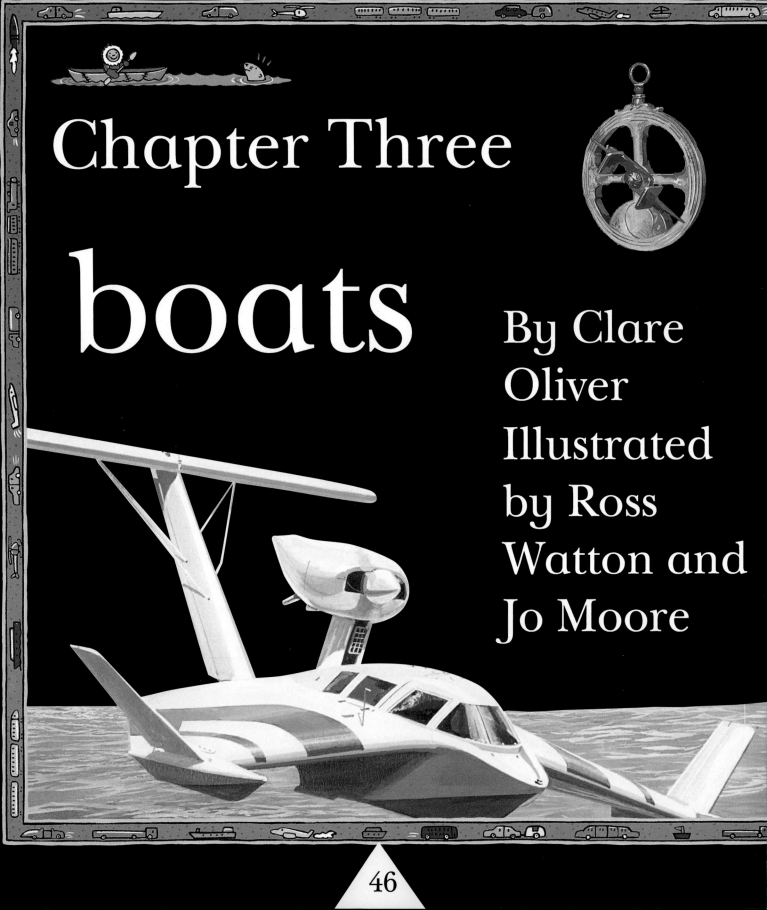

Chapter Three

boats

By Clare Oliver

Illustrated by Ross Watton and Jo Moore

Introduction

Discover for yourself the most amazing facts about boats, ships, and submarines from the earliest boats to the massive cruise liners that carry nearly 4,000 passengers.

Did you know that it took 170 Greeks to row a boat? ... that ships found a new world? ... that ships sailed on air? ... that some warships are made of plastic? ... that you can swim on a ship? ... that some boats sink on purpose? ... that some ships are like airports? ... that some boats are unsinkable? ... that some boats have wings?

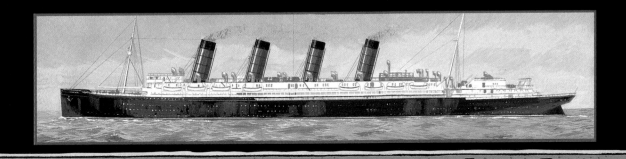

I didn't know that

it took 170 Greeks to row a boat. On the open sea, sails powered Greek warships. The trireme's men saved their strength for battle. Then they rowed at top speed into the enemy. The bronze battering ram on the bow could punch a hole in the enemy's ship to sink her.

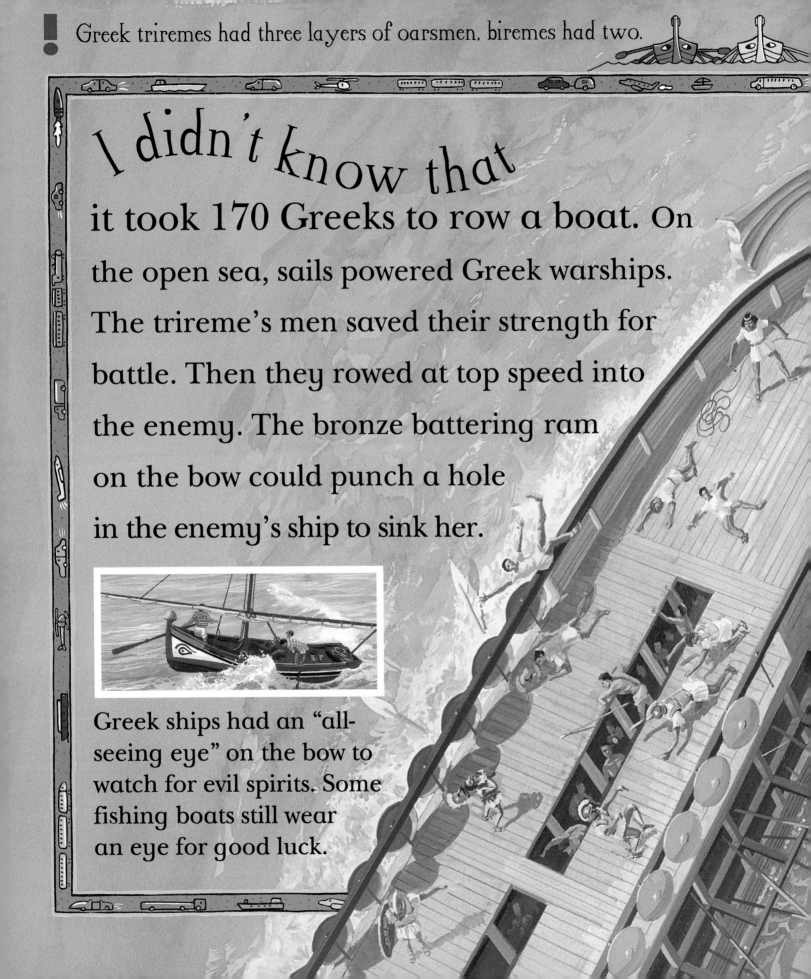

Greek ships had an "all-seeing eye" on the bow to watch for evil spirits. Some fishing boats still wear an eye for good luck.

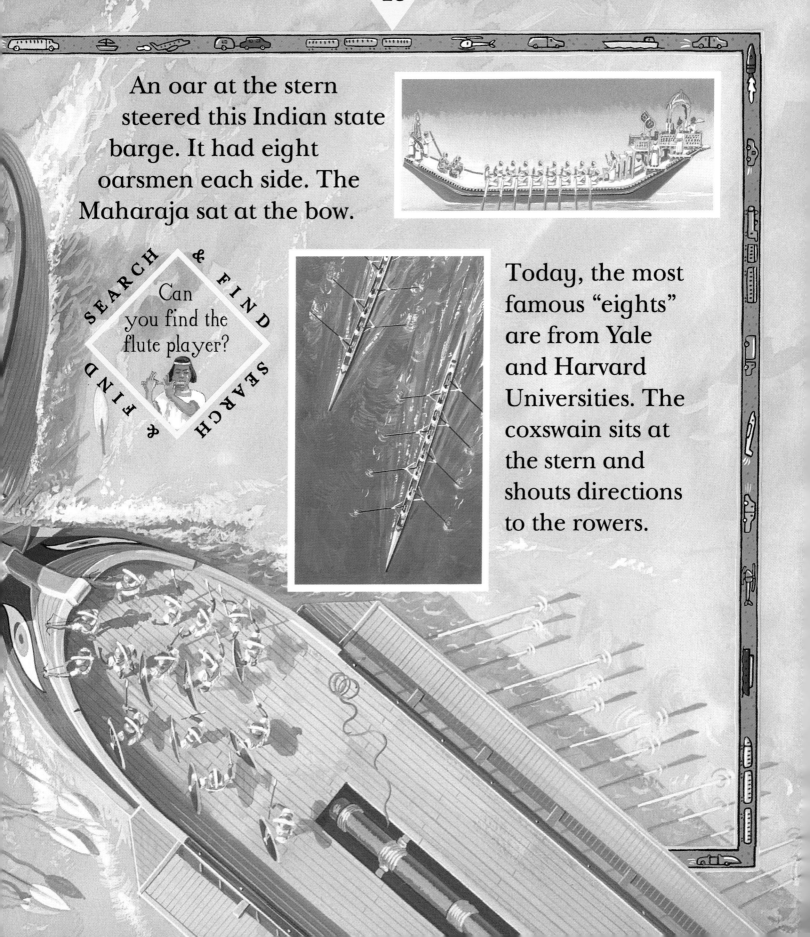

An oar at the stern steered this Indian state barge. It had eight oarsmen each side. The Maharaja sat at the bow.

SEARCH & FIND & FIND SEARCH &

Can you find the flute player?

Today, the most famous "eights" are from Yale and Harvard Universities. The coxswain sits at the stern and shouts directions to the rowers.

I didn't know that

ships found a New World.

In the 1400s, explorers set sail in ships called caravels. Christopher Columbus, looking for a route to India, found America. He called the islands he came to the West Indies.

An astrolabe measured the height and position of the sun and stars. Using this sailors could chart their position at sea.

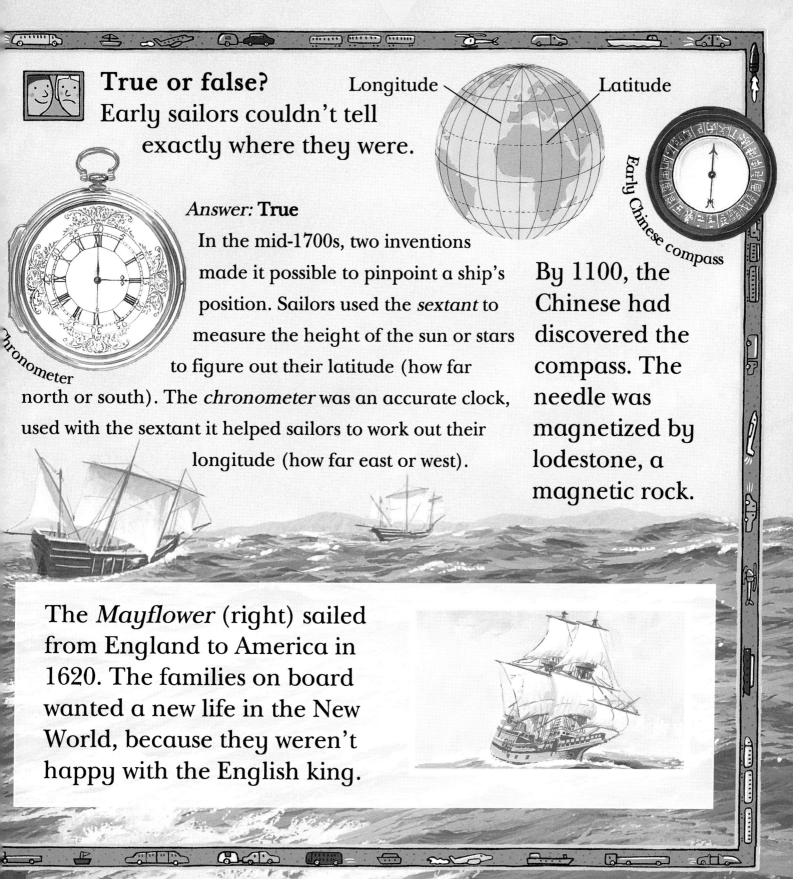

True or false?
Early sailors couldn't tell exactly where they were.

Longitude

Latitude

Early Chinese compass

Answer: **True**

In the mid-1700s, two inventions made it possible to pinpoint a ship's position. Sailors used the *sextant* to measure the height of the sun or stars to figure out their latitude (how far north or south). The *chronometer* was an accurate clock, used with the sextant it helped sailors to work out their longitude (how far east or west).

Chronometer

By 1100, the Chinese had discovered the compass. The needle was magnetized by lodestone, a magnetic rock.

The *Mayflower* (right) sailed from England to America in 1620. The families on board wanted a new life in the New World, because they weren't happy with the English king.

Ferdinand Magellan led the first expedition that sailed around the world.

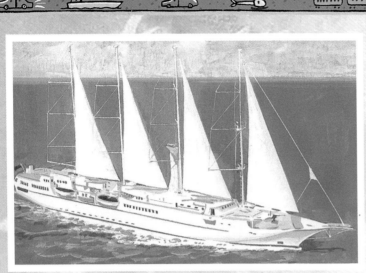

Some modern liners (left) are returning to sail power. They can turn off their engines on ocean voyages to cut down on fuel and pollution.

SEARCH & FIND

Can you find two seagulls?

FIND & SEARCH

Yachts are sailing ships used for pleasure and racing. The world's most famous sailboat competition is the America's Cup.

True or false?

A ship's speed is measured in knots.

Answer: **True**

One knot equals one nautical mile. Early explorers tied a float to a rope with evenly spaced knots. They would throw the float into the sea and count how many knots unraveled into the sea in the time it took an hourglass to empty.

Clippers could beat steamships - if the winds were good!

The *Cutty Sark*'s figurehead wore a cutty sark (linen shirt).

I didn't know that

ships sailed on air. With the wind in her sails, a clipper such as the *Cutty Sark* could travel along at 17 knots on air-power alone. This merchant ship had 34 sails and could get a *cargo* of tea from China to London in 110 days.

This clipper's narrow hull (above) could slide through a bottle neck. The hinged mast and sails were pulled up with a wire.

True or false?

You could be forced to join the Navy.

Answer: **True**

The low pay, appalling conditions, and long service made going to sea unpopular. So navies used Press Gangs. They were groups of tough sailors who kidnapped men and forced them onto the ships.

Ironclads (right) were the first ships to wear armor. The first battle between ironclads took place in 1862 during the U.S. Civil War. Neither the *Monitor* nor the *Merrimack* came out a clear winner.

The American ship *USS Constitution* had a copper bottom! The metal protected the hull from wood-eating shellfish. It also stopped weeds from growing there thus reducing the boat's *drag* in the water.

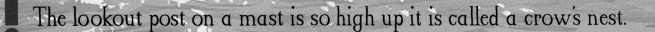

The lookout post on a mast is so high up it is called a crow's nest.

I didn't know that

some warships are made of plastic. Engine noise or a hull's magnetic pull can set off mines. Minesweepers clear underwater bombs (mines). They have silent engines and some have plastic, non-magnetic hulls.

SEARCH & FIND
FIND & SEARCH
Can you find the mine?

HMS Middleton
(a "Hunt" class, plastic-hulled minesweeper)

M34

55

I didn't know that

you can swim on a ship. *Carnival Destiny*, a Caribbean cruise ship, has four swimming pools on board! One pool has a slide 213 ft above sea level and another has a glass roof that slides open.

Most huge liners rely on tugboats and pilots to pull and steer them carefully into the dock. Not the *Destiny*! She can be docked using a joystick in the control room.

! Fast, cheap jumbo jets took over from the luxury liners.

SEARCH & FIND Can you find the pool slide? FIND & SEARCH

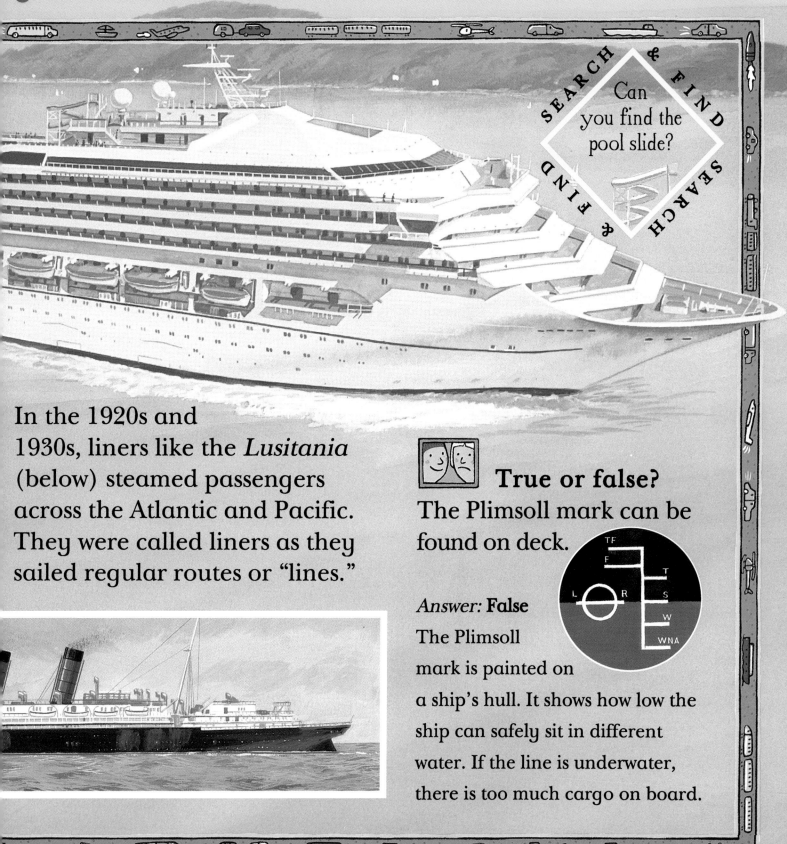

In the 1920s and 1930s, liners like the *Lusitania* (below) steamed passengers across the Atlantic and Pacific. They were called liners as they sailed regular routes or "lines."

True or false?
The Plimsoll mark can be found on deck.

Answer: **False**
The Plimsoll mark is painted on a ship's hull. It shows how low the ship can safely sit in different water. If the line is underwater, there is too much cargo on board.

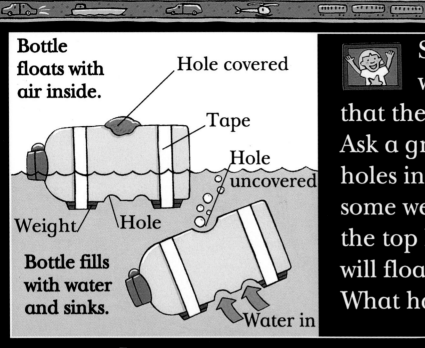

Bottle floats with air inside.

Hole covered

Tape

Hole uncovered

Weight | Hole

Bottle fills with water and sinks.

Water in

Subs have tanks that let water or air in and out so that they can sink or resurface. Ask a grown-up to cut three holes in a plastic bottle. Tape on some weights, like coins. Cover the top hole with clay. The sub will float. Take off the top cover. What happens to the sub?

Alvin

I didn't know that

some boats sink on purpose.

Submarines and submersibles are designed to sink. Submarines are used to sneak up on enemy targets without being seen. Submersibles are much smaller and are used to explore the deep. In 1986, *Alvin* was used to explore the wreck of the *Titanic*, 9,000 ft down on the seabed.

Trieste made the deepest-ever dive – to nearly 36,000 ft.

The *Turtle* was built in 1776. There was room for one person inside, who was kept busy turning the propellers by hand.

The biggest and fastest submarines are the six *nuclear-powered* Russian *Typhoons* (above). These massive missile machines can top 40 knots. Military submarines cruise the oceans constantly to keep the peace.

Turtle

Titanic

I didn't know that

some ships are like airports. Massive aircraft carriers can carry over 70 fighter planes at once! The deck is a mini runway.

The biggest ship ever is *Jahre Viking,* a supertanker. As long as four football fields, she weighs more than 1,000 jumbo jets!

USS Nimitz

NAVY

 True or false?
Ships can give piggyback rides.

Answer: **True**
A heavy-lift ship (right) lowers herself in the water so the smaller ship can float aboard, then she rises with the smaller ship on deck.

SEARCH & FIND • FIND SEARCH & FIND SEARCH &
Can you find three helicopters?

An icebreaker (below) cuts through frozen seas to carve a path for other ships to follow.

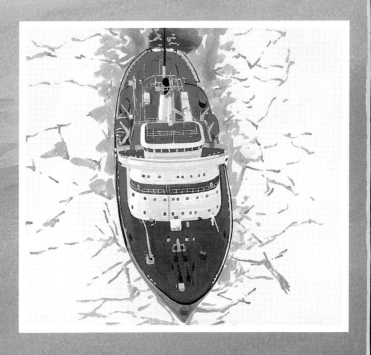

Ships like aircraft carriers, icebreakers, and some submarines are nuclear powered. Nuclear power allows them to stay at sea for very long periods without having to refuel.

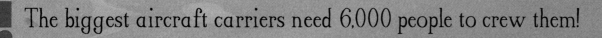

The biggest aircraft carriers need 6,000 people to crew them!

I didn't know that

some boats are unsinkable.

Well, almost! Because lifeboats usually go to sea in dangerous conditions, they can sometimes run into trouble themselves. If a big wave turns the boat over, special *buoyancy tanks* turn the boat the right way up almost immediately.

SEARCH & FIND
Can you find the man overboard?
FIND & SEARCH &

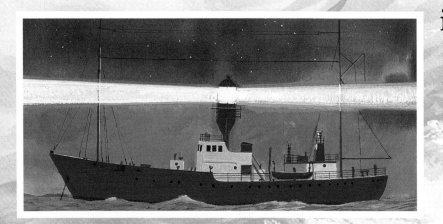

A light ship is like a floating lighthouse with a beacon that can be seen from about 24 miles away. She stays anchored in a dangerous spot to warn other ships.

The ocean liner *Titanic* (right) was supposed to be unsinkable. Disaster struck when she hit an iceberg on her maiden (first) voyage – and sank.

Some lifeguards use special rowboats (right) to patrol the beaches for swimmers caught by high waves.

In 1997, Tony Bullimore survived 89 hours inside the hull of his yacht.

A hovercraft floats on a cushion of air trapped inside her "skirt." As she doesn't drag in the water she can beat most ships.

I didn't know that

some boats have wings. It's hard to tell whether a wingship is a boat or a plane! At high speeds its hull is lifted 6 ft above the surface of the water. With their turned-up tips, the wings create a pocket of air for the wingship to coast along on.

Some vehicles, such as the *Half-Safe*, go on land and water.

Catamarans have two hulls (right). With less boat in the water they are much faster than ordinary boats. With two hulls for support, they are steadier in rough seas.

The new twin-hulled yacht, *Goss Challenger* (above), built for The Race in 2000, is expected to beat the around-the-world record.

True or false?
Some ships squirt water.

Answer: **True**
Catamarans use water-jets to propel themselves forward. New cargo ships called fastships will use water-jets and be twice as fast as today's cargo ships.

Chapter Four
trucks

By William Petty

Illustrated by Ross Watton and Jo Moore

Introduction

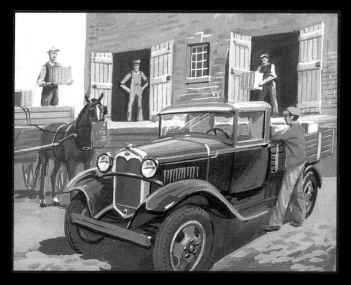

Discover for yourself amazing facts about trucks. Learn about all types of trucks from the earliest steam-powered ones to today's hi-tech models.

Did you know that trucks used to run on steam? ... that a truck can be as big as a house? ... that some fire trucks have a driver at each end? ... that some trucks can swim? ... that modern trucks drive on air? ... that a truck can carry a spacecraft? ... that you can find trucks at a race track?

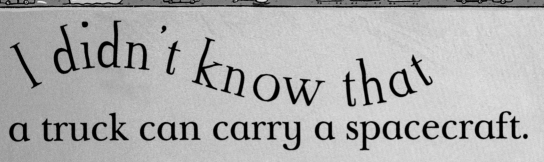

I didn't know that

a truck can carry a spacecraft.

This truck carries space shuttles to the launch site. Its enormous trailer can carry the weight of a 68-ton craft! The police have to close the roads and escort it.

 True or false?
A truck can carry a nuclear missile.

Answer: **True**
This truck is towing a nuclear missile as part of a parade. The heavy missile is not armed, but it must still be loaded very carefully.

This gas storage vessel was the longest load ever, at 275 feet long! The truck's route was planned months in advance to avoid narrow roads and tight corners. The journey took place early in the morning when the roads were less busy.

The army uses trucks like this one (below) to transport tanks over long distances by road. Tanks are ideal for crossing rough, off-road terrain, but their hard metal tracks can damage road surfaces.

One hundred years ago, trucks competed with horses for business. In the 1920s, Ford advertised trucks with the slogan, "It doesn't need feeding when standing still," unlike hungry horses!

True or false?
There was a truck more than 200 years ago.

Answer: **True**
In 1769 Nicolas-Joseph Cugnot built a steam tractor to pull cannons into battle (below). It went out of control during testing and was abandoned.

Rudolf Diesel invented the diesel engine in 1897. Today most trucks are powered by a diesel engine and diesel fuel.

I didn't know that trucks used to run on steam. Before the gasoline engine became widely used, trucks were powered by steam. Water heated in a boiler became steam and turned the wheels. Today, steam is not used in trucks.

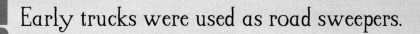

Early trucks were used as road sweepers.

Trailers are supported by "feet" when they're not attached to a cab.

True or false?

Trucks can bend.

Answer: **True**
Articulated trucks bend where the cab is connected to the trailer. This means that they can turn corners more easily.

Fifth wheel

Trucks can carry a lot of cargo. A fork-lift truck (right) is useful for loading and unloading. Its movable prongs at the front mean it can lift heavy objects onto or off a truck.

Can you find the four wrenches?

I didn't know that

some trucks have a fifth wheel. The "fifth wheel" is the device that connects a tractor to its trailer. It acts like a hinge. Because the trailer can be detached, it can be easily moved from one tractor unit to another.

This funny-looking contraption was the world's first-ever articulated vehicle, *Thornycroft*. It was built in Britain in 1897, over 100 years ago. Although the gasoline engine had been invented by then, *Thornycroft* still ran on steam.

I didn't know that

a truck can be as big as a house. The Terex Titan has a 16-cylinder engine and can carry an incredible 350 tons! It is too big to travel by road and has to be assembled on-site.

Can you find five yellow hard hats?
SEARCH & FIND & SEARCH & FIND

You can see concrete mixers like this one (left) on the highway. The drum has to turn all the time, or else the wet concrete in the mixer will harden and set.

Cranes like this (right) are used on building sites to move heavy objects. The extending arm can lift things to great heights.

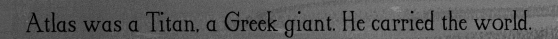

Atlas was a Titan, a Greek giant. He carried the world.

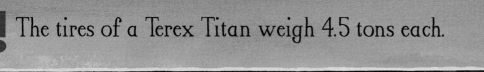

True or false?
Some trucks have tracks.

Answer: **True**
Some trucks are specially fitted with
Caterpillar tracks — just like a bulldozer!
They can drive over bumpy
ground.

Trucks carrying dangerous substances display warning signs. They are international; no language is used. Guess what sort of dangers these four signs describe. The pictures should tell you. Try making up your own signs.

A Flammable, B Radioactive, C Explosive, D Corrosive

A

B

C

D

Can you find the chocolate bar?

SEARCH & FIND SEARCH & FIND

Tankers are used to remove blockages from road drains.

Scientists are now developing *"green" fuels,* such as alcohol made from plant sap. In Brazil, the high cost of fuel led to the development of a car that runs on plant alcohol.

I didn't know that tankers can be filled with chocolate. Tankers transport all kinds of liquids. They carry fuels for cars and airplanes, as well as liquid food and drink — including liquid chocolate!

Most tankers are divided up into several separate compartments inside. This makes them more stable, and means that one tanker can carry loads for different customers.

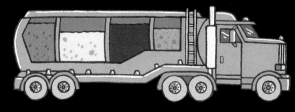

Firefighters use fire truck ladders (left) to reach the tops of buildings. The ladder can stretch to 100 feet long and can carry 1,500 pounds, even in a strong wind!

Specially designed fire trucks (right) work at airports, where a fire could be disastrous. When a plane has to make an emergency landing, they spray foam on the runway.

I didn't know that

some fire trucks have a driver at each end. The articulated Aerial Tiller fire truck has a second cab at the back. The firefighter who sits there can steer the truck through winding streets.

The Aerial Tiller's ladder carries a powerful 1,500-foot hose that delivers 1,000 gallons of water per minute. When the ladder is up, stabilizers extend out from each side to help balance the truck.

Stabilizers stop a fire truck from falling over.

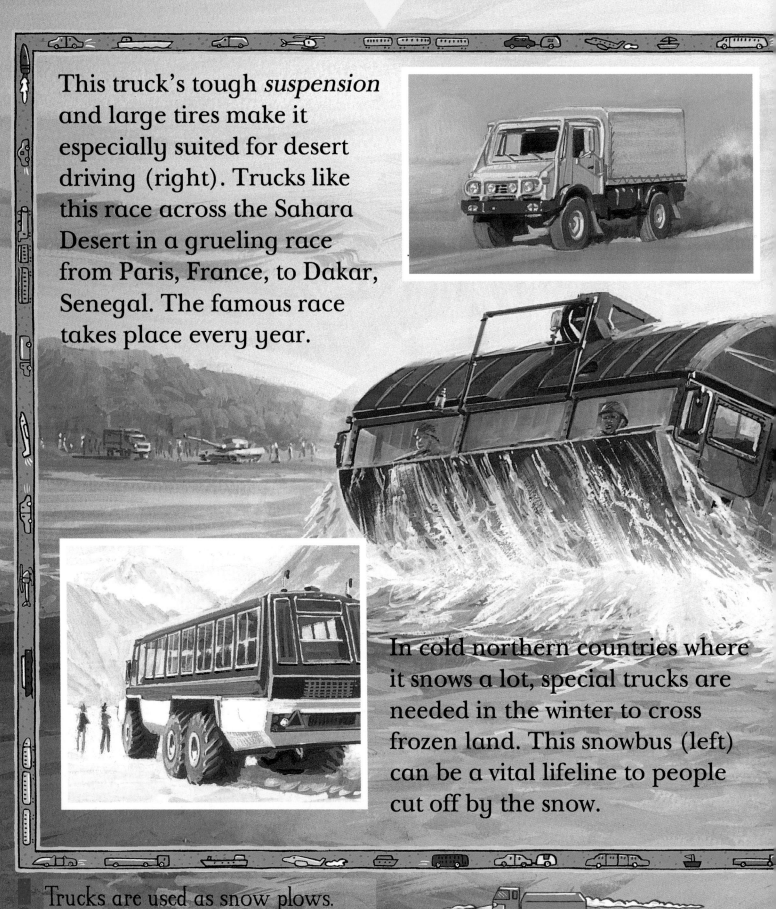

This truck's tough *suspension* and large tires make it especially suited for desert driving (right). Trucks like this race across the Sahara Desert in a grueling race from Paris, France, to Dakar, Senegal. The famous race takes place every year.

In cold northern countries where it snows a lot, special trucks are needed in the winter to cross frozen land. This snowbus (left) can be a vital lifeline to people cut off by the snow.

Trucks are used as snow plows.

I didn't know that

some trucks can swim.
This army truck is amphibious
— it can travel on land or in water.
The engine turns wheels and a propeller.
Its flat top means it can form a bridge to
transport other vehicles over water.

Snow chains fitted to a tire like this give a truck or a car the extra grip it needs to drive across ice and snow without skidding.

I didn't know that

Juggernaut is a god. Enormous trucks are called juggernauts, after a Hindu god. In Puri, India, people used to throw themselves under the wheels of the giant cart that carried a statue of the god.

SEARCH & FIND & FIND & SEARCH

Can you find three teddy bears?

This crane is loading a *container* onto a truck. Because the containers are detachable, they can be moved from trucks to boats or trains and back easily. They can also be stored neatly.

In countries where there are few railroads, such as Australia, "road trains" like this one above carry goods over long distances. Road trains consist of three or four trailers linked together. The longest-ever road train was the length of 16 cars!

Trucks were banned from the first U.S. freeway in 1925.

I didn't know that

modern trucks drive on air.
Today's hi-tech trucks are equipped
with *compressed air* tanks. High-pressure
air at work in the brake and suspension
systems ensures fast braking
and a smooth ride.

SEARCH & FIND

Can you find the road runner?

FIND & SEARCH

In the future, all
trucks might look
like this! They will
be made with new materials — lighter and
stronger than those of today. They will also
produce less pollution than older trucks.

Fuel tank

Some trucks have as many as 22 wheels.

This truck (left) is being tested in a *wind tunnel* to find out how *aerodynamic* it is — how easily it cuts through the air. A sleek, streamlined truck requires less power to move it forward.

Aerodynamic driver's quarters

Driver's cab

True or false?
Some truck cabs flip up.

Answer: **True**
Some truck cabs flip up so mechanics can check the engine underneath. Trucks that flip like this are called cab-over units.

Have you ever seen a truck like this one (left)? "Monster trucks" are normal trucks but with huge wheels, powerful engines, and strong suspension. They are big enough to crush ordinary cars under their tires! Watch for monster truck shows near you!

This truck (above) has been customized. It has been given a special paint job, and some parts have been replaced. This means the truck is unique — each one is different!

I didn't know that

you can find trucks on a race track. Skilled drivers race trucks in competitions. They give them extra-powerful engines — great for high-speed driving! Racing trucks are made of lightweight materials.

 True or false?
Trucks can do stunts.

Answer: **True**
This truck is doing a wheelie. It has to have a lot of power in its back wheels to do this.

Some monster trucks can weigh more than 10 tons.

Chapter Five

cars

By
William
Petty

Illustrated by
Gerald Witcomb and
Don Simpson

Introduction

Discover for yourself the
most amazing facts about
cars from the most

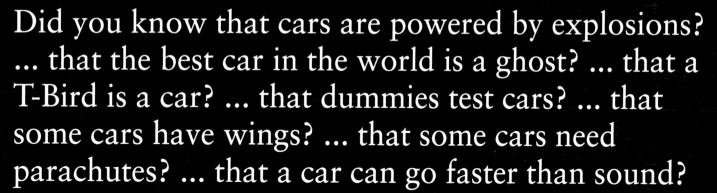

expensive car in the world to the latest
computer-controlled vehicles.

Did you know that cars are powered by explosions?
... that the best car in the world is a ghost? ... that a
T-Bird is a car? ... that dummies test cars? ... that
some cars have wings? ... that some cars need
parachutes? ... that a car can go faster than sound?

... that some cars can
swim? ... that some cars
have two engines?

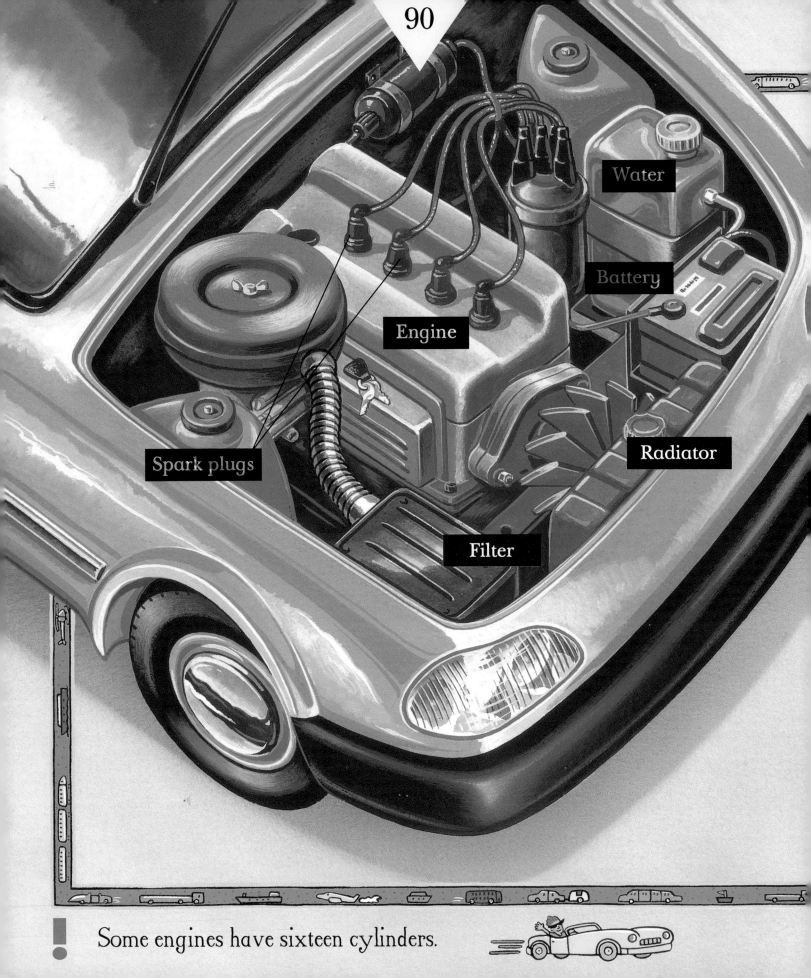

Water

Battery

Engine

Radiator

Spark plugs

Filter

Some engines have sixteen cylinders.

I didn't know that

cars are powered by explosions. Inside a car's engine gasoline mixed with air is exploded. This force pushes the pistons, driving the engine.

True or false?
All cars have engines under the hood.

Answer: **False**
Some, such as the Volkswagen Beetle and the Fiat Seicento, have the engine in the trunk! Under the hood there is space for luggage.

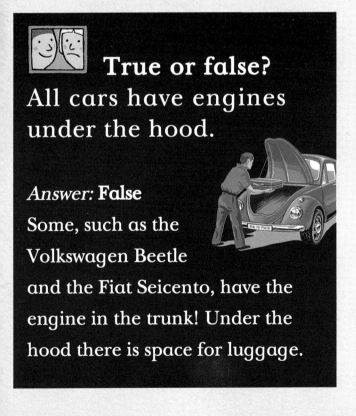

The spark plugs create the sparks that ignite the mixture of gasoline and air in the engine. The battery starts the engine and supplies power to other electrical systems. Air for the engine is cleaned by a filter and water cools the engine using the radiator.

I didn't know that

the best car in the world is a ghost.

The Rolls Royce Silver Ghost is renowned for its superb engine and its stylish looks. Many people believe it is the best car in the world.

The stylish 1935 Auburn Speedster was perfect for cruising around glamourous Hollywood. Each car came with a plaque certifying that it had been driven at over 99 miles per hour by racing driver Ab Jenkins.

The most expensive car ever was the enormous Bugatti Royale – it was 22 feet long! Only six of them were ever made. In 1990, a Royale was sold at auction for $15 million.

One of the greatest Grand Prix cars of all was the 1937 Mercedes W125. With the help of two enormous superchargers, it reached speeds of almost 198.4 miles per hour!

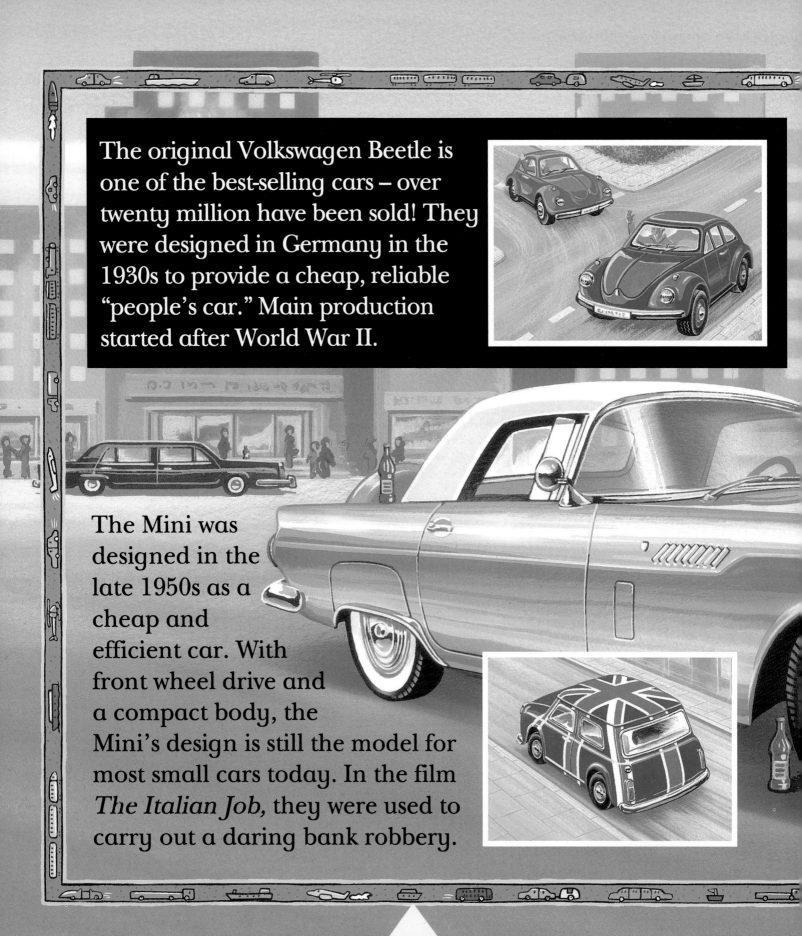

The original Volkswagen Beetle is one of the best-selling cars – over twenty million have been sold! They were designed in Germany in the 1930s to provide a cheap, reliable "people's car." Main production started after World War II.

The Mini was designed in the late 1950s as a cheap and efficient car. With front wheel drive and a compact body, the Mini's design is still the model for most small cars today. In the film *The Italian Job,* they were used to carry out a daring bank robbery.

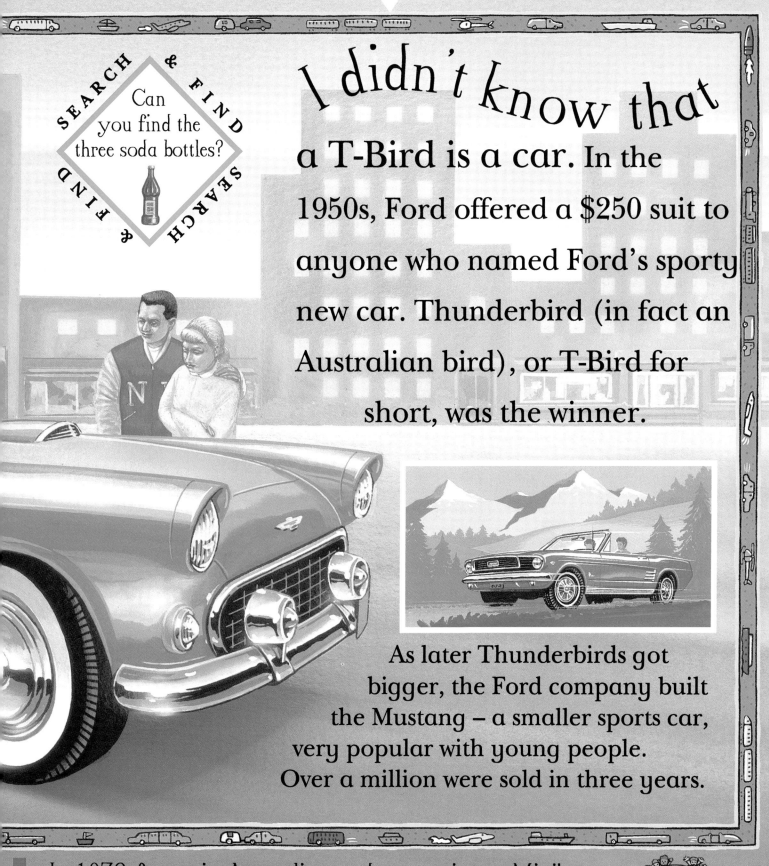

I didn't know that

a T-Bird is a car. In the 1950s, Ford offered a $250 suit to anyone who named Ford's sporty new car. Thunderbird (in fact an Australian bird), or T-Bird for short, was the winner.

As later Thunderbirds got bigger, the Ford company built the Mustang – a smaller sports car, very popular with young people. Over a million were sold in three years.

In 1972, forty-six Australian students got in one Mini!

I didn't know that

dummies test cars. New cars undergo a series of safety tests. Dummies, accurate models of humans, are used to see how the car behaves in a series of crash situations.

SEARCH & FIND

Can you find the crash test bear?

Early brakes often failed.

Many different types of crashes are simulated. Cars have to protect passengers from front and side impacts. Airbags (right) in the front and sides are fully tested.

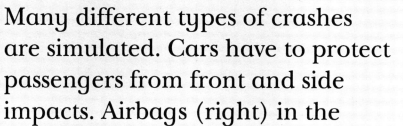

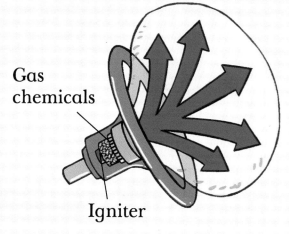

Gas chemicals

Igniter

Chemicals will inflate an airbag in forty milliseconds. This is less than a third of the time it takes to blink!

 True or false?
Some cars are armor-plated.

Answer: **True**
This Zil limousine, used by Russian presidents, could

be the safest car in the world! It weighs 6.6 tons and is covered with 3-inch-thick steel armor plating.

Every year, drivers compete in up to sixteen Formula One Grand Prix races around the world. Each race is at least 186 miles long. Monaco is a difficult race, where drivers have to negotiate narrow city streets at high speed.

Formula One cars need to have different types of tires for wet and dry weather. Normally the tires are changed mid-race.

Racing tire

Wet-weather tire

I didn't know that

some cars have wings.

Formula One cars go at above 186 miles per hour and are designed with upside-down wings, which push the car downward. This helps them to grip the track.

True or false?

You can change tires in seconds.

Answer: **True**

During a race drivers can pull into the pit-lane to change tires, re-fuel or for minor repairs. Pit-crew mechanics are trained to change tires and add fuel in seconds.

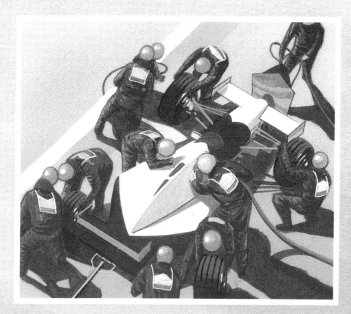

 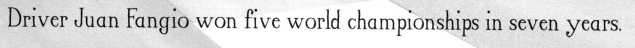 Driver Juan Fangio won five world championships in seven years.

I didn't know that

some cars need parachutes.
Dragsters can reach speeds of
200 miles per hour in less than five
seconds! They go so fast on a short
track that they need parachutes to
slow them down.

SEARCH & FIND & SEARCH & FIND

Can you find the oil can?

Rally cars are based
on road cars. Rally cars are
prepared to race against the
clock over roads, mud, gravel,
snow, and ice. The driver
and the navigator, who gives
directions, are protected by
a steel safety cage.

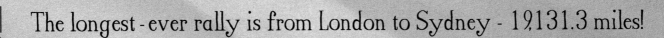

The longest - ever rally is from London to Sydney - 19,131.3 miles!

At Le Mans, cars race for 24 hours only stopping to change drivers, re-fuel or have minor repairs. The race used to begin with drivers running to their cars, but this was abandoned because it was too dangerous.

To see how a parachute will help to slow down a speeding car, attach a piece of string to each corner of a hankie. Fasten the ends of the strings to a ball of clay. Throw it high into the air.

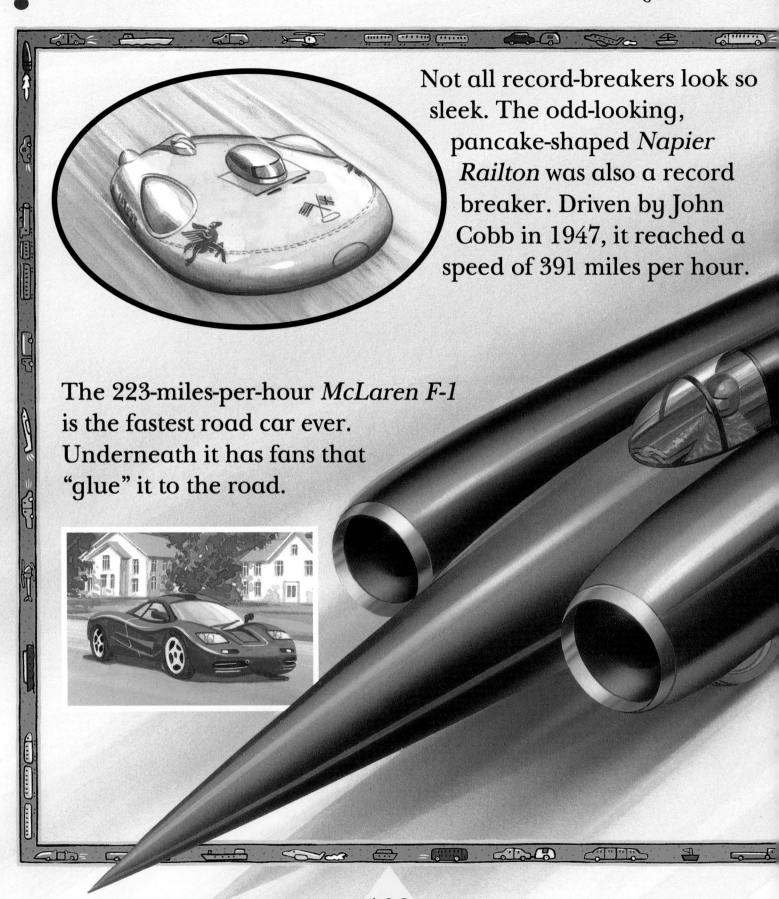

When *Thrust SCC* broke the sound barrier there was a loud bang.

Not all record-breakers look so sleek. The odd-looking, pancake-shaped *Napier Railton* was also a record breaker. Driven by John Cobb in 1947, it reached a speed of 391 miles per hour.

The 223-miles-per-hour *McLaren F-1* is the fastest road car ever. Underneath it has fans that "glue" it to the road.

I didn't know that a car can go faster than sound. In October 1997, *Thrust SCC* became the first car to break the *sound barrier*. In Black Rock, Nevada, it reached an incredible 764.8 miles per hour!

Donald Campbell broke the land-speed record in 1964, reaching speeds of 430 miles per hour in his gas-powered *Bluebird* car.

 In 1994 an electric car traveled at 186 miles per hour.

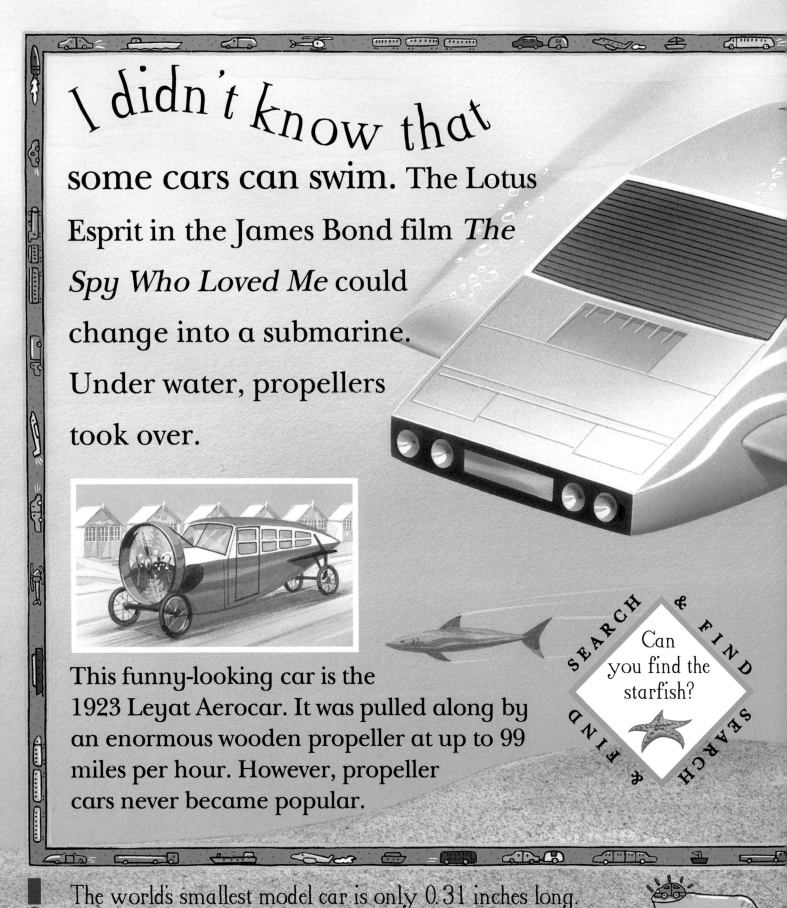

I didn't know that

some cars can swim. The Lotus Esprit in the James Bond film *The Spy Who Loved Me* could change into a submarine. Under water, propellers took over.

This funny-looking car is the 1923 Leyat Aerocar. It was pulled along by an enormous wooden propeller at up to 99 miles per hour. However, propeller cars never became popular.

SEARCH & FIND & FIND SEARCH & SEARCH

Can you find the starfish?

The world's smallest model car is only 0.31 inches long.

! The Grosser Mercedes, used by the German Army, had six wheels.

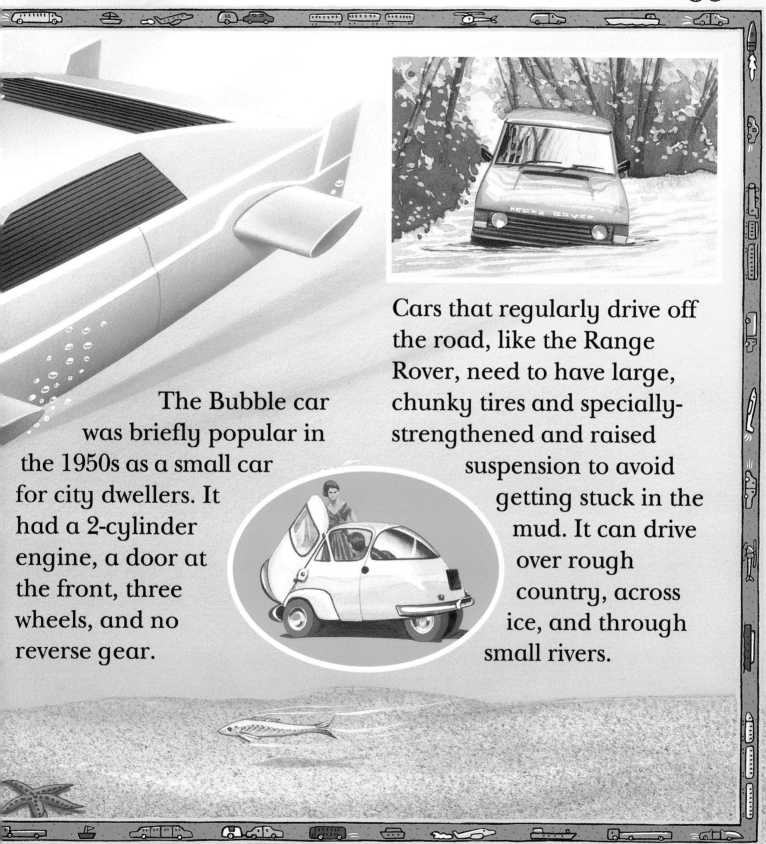

Cars that regularly drive off the road, like the Range Rover, need to have large, chunky tires and specially-strengthened and raised suspension to avoid getting stuck in the mud. It can drive over rough country, across ice, and through small rivers.

The Bubble car was briefly popular in the 1950s as a small car for city dwellers. It had a 2-cylinder engine, a door at the front, three wheels, and no reverse gear.

I didn't know that

some cars have two engines.
The Toyota Prius has an electric engine for low speeds, and a gasoline engine that kicks in when the car reaches a higher speed.

SEARCH & FIND
Can you find five rabbits?

This car has been fitted with a *solar panel* on the roof that absorbs heat energy from the sun and converts it into electricity. Cars like this need a hot climate. In Australia, there is a race from Darwin to Adelaide that is exclusively for solar-powered cars.

Some cars are entirely driven by electric motors. They are better for the environment, but they are expensive to run and have a very short range.

 Some London taxis in 1896 were electric powered.

Glossary

Aerodynamic
A shape which cuts through air easily.

Ailerons, elevators and rudder
Movable panels on wings, tailplane, and tail for tilting and turning the plane.

Airfoil
Wing shape best suited to giving lift. The airflow is faster over the curved surface so air pressure above is lower than air pressure below.

Articulated
Built in connected sections. Helps long vehicles to go around bends more easily.

Biplane
Plane with two sets of wings, one above the other.

Buoyancy tanks
Containers that are filled with air. These make lifeboats float very high in the water and stop them from sinking in high seas.

Cargo
The load carried by a vehicle.

Caterpillar tracks
Wide belts made of metal or rubber plates, driven by cogs, that are used instead of wheels on some heavy vehicles.

Chronometer
An instrument that lets us work out longitude by measuring time.

Compressed air
Air squashed into a small space. Compressed air expands if allowed to, so it can push machine parts.

Conductor rail
Electrified rail that passes electricity to an electric train.

Container
A big box, usually of steel, for carrying a cargo.

Cylinder
A hollow tube inside an engine in which a gas is ignited and expands to push a piston.

Diesel-electric
On diesel-electric trains the diesel engine powers a generator that provides electricity for the motor.

Drag
Water pressing against a boat's hull produces a force called drag which slows the boat down.

"Green" fuel
A fuel which gives off less harmful gases. Green fuels, like seaweed, are renewable – they can be grown or produced. They should not therefore run out.

Ironclad
Warship of the 19th century that was covered in protective iron plates.

Jet
In a jet engine air is sucked in, mixed with fuel, ignited and forced out in a jet that moves the aircraft forwards.

Lift
Force that keeps an airplane up, created when the air pressure below is higher than the air pressure above the wing.

Mach 1
The speed of sound, named after physicist Ernst Mach. Mach 2 is twice the speed of sound.

Maglev
Short for "magnetic levitation". A train that is moved and lifted along above the track by magnetic forces.

Nuclear power
Some ships travel farther with less fuel by using tiny amounts of powerful radioactive fuels to make steam power.

Pantographs
The metal frames on top of an electric train that pick up the electric current from overhead wires.

Piston
The disk that moves inside the cylinder, attached to a rod that turns a crankshaft or flywheel.

Propeller
Blades that rotate in air or water to move a plane or a boat along.

Radar

Stands for RAdio Detection And Ranging, used for detecting objects by bouncing radio waves off them.

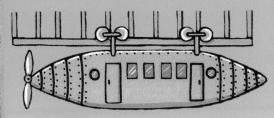

Ramjet

Type of engine that can provide extra power only when the aircraft is moving.

Rotor

Rotating blade that breaks up airflow to give lift.

Sextant

An instrument that lets us work out our position on the earth's surface by measuring the position of the sun and the stars.

Solar panel

A device which collects energy from the sun's rays and turns it into electric energy for heating or driving an engine.

Sound barrier

Any vehicle which travels faster than sound waves move through the air (about 1083 feet per second at ground level) is said to have broken the sound barrier.

Supersonic

Faster than the speed of sound. A supersonic aircraft breaking the sound barrier makes a "sonic boom" as shock waves reach the ground.

Suspension

A system of springs or other devices that smooth out the ride in a vehicle.

TACV

Tracked Air Cushion Vehicle – one that moves on a cushion of air above a track.

Thrust

The force that pushes a craft forwards.

Wind tunnel

A machine that blows air over a vehicle. Using computers, it then shows scientists how the air flows over the surfaces.

Index

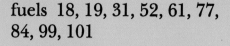

Index

Mach 1 17, 18, 109
Magellan, Ferdinand 51
Maglev 43, 109
monorail 42, 43

Napier Railton 102
nuclear power 59, 61, 109

Panavia Tornado 20, 21

pantographs 38, 109
parachutes 100, 101
passengers 9, 14, 16, 17, 41, 57, 97
pilots 16, 26, 27, 56
pistons 30, 91, 109
Plimsoll mark 57
pollution 44, 52, 84
power 24, 30, 34, 38, 39, 42, 44, 53, 85, 87
propellers 9, 22, 35, 42, 59, 81, 104, 109

rack and pinion 33
radars 20, 110
rails 30, 33, 38, 39, 42, 44
ramjets 17, 110
rockets 18, 19
Rolls Royce 92
rotors 22, 23, 24, 110
rowing 48, 49, 63
rudder 27, 108

sails 48, 52, 53
seaplanes 14, 15
sextant 51, 110
Silver Bullet 16
sound barrier 102, 103, 110
Space Shuttle 10, 68
speed of sound 17, 110
Spirit of Australia 65
steam 8, 12, 30, 32, 33, 35, 38, 52, 70, 71, 73
streamlined 32, 85
submarines 58, 59, 61, 104
supersonic 17, 18, 110
suspension 80, 84, 86, 100, 105, 110

TACV 42, 110

tankers 60, 76, 77
TGV 40, 41
Thornycroft 73
thrust 19, 27, 110
Thrust SCC 17, 102, 103
Thunderbirds 95
tires 75, 80, 81, 86, 99, 105
Titanic 58, 59, 63
tractors 70, 73
Trieste 58

VTOL 24

warships 48, 55
wheels 14, 30, 32, 33, 34, 42, 71, 72, 81, 82, 84, 86, 87, 91, 105
wheel combination 32
wind 22, 52, 85
wind tunnel 85, 110
wings 11, 12, 18, 20, 21, 26, 64, 99
wires 27, 38, 39, 44, 53
Wright brothers 10, 12